SECRETS
OF
# VERSAILLES

# SECRETS
## OF
# VERSAILLES

## THE PALACE AND BEYOND

NICOLAS BRUNO JACQUET
TRANSLATED BY LILITH COWAN

This book wouldn't have come to be without the invaluable support of the following people, to whom I wish to express my gratitude. First of all, thanks to Jean-Jacques Aillagon, Former President of the Établissement Public du Musée et du Domaine National de Versailles (EPV), who threw open the doors of the palace for me. I'm also grateful to Jean-Vincent Bacquart, in charge of publishing for the EPV, his colleague Anne Déon, and Émilie Jacques, who supported me all along the way. Thanks to Bruno Archinard for his insatiable curiosity and his talent, to Grégory Pouchkine, François Besse, and Laurence Solnais for their attentiveness and generosity, and to the whole team at Parigramme.
I would like to express my gratitude in particular to Claude Loupiac, who gave me the benefit of his wisdom.
Finally, thanks to the many enthusiastic guide-lecturers and to all those who introduced me to the hidden treasures of the palace of Versailles and its environs.

Asterisks are used as follows to indicate the sites presented in this work that are subject to restricted access:
* guided tours only,
** closed to the public.

# TABLE OF CONTENTS

# FOREWORD

Versailles is one of the best-known heritage sites in the world. The palace and its grounds are high in the Top Ten, alongside the pyramids of Egypt, the Parthenon in Athens, the Taj Mahal, the Forbidden City in Beijing, and a few other iconic monuments.

It is for this reason that many people think they already know everything there is to know about Versailles, although the palace and its annexes cover over 200,000 square meters, and many secrets and mysteries remain tucked away in its nearly 1,000 hectares of grounds.

This work, penned by Nicolas Jacquet, aims to provide readers with the keys to some of these closed doors, helping them to infiltrate solid walls and transporting them beyond appearances to tap into some of the secret and unexpected aspects of the heritage and history of the palace of Louis XIV and his successors. Louis-Philippe turned the palace into a Museum of the History of France; today, it is a national monument and a UNESCO World Heritage Site.

May readers understand that, behind the façades and the decors of the most beautiful palace in France, you can still sense the beating hearts of the men and women who once inhabited it and the history that unfolded there.

May they also understand that this palace is neither a dead site nor a placid memorial, but rather a living space which still aims to surprise and amaze visitors and fill them with wonder.

I thank the author for inviting us there with finesse, erudition, and sensitivity.

JEAN-JACQUES AILLAGON

# INTRODUCTION

"Delos, grant my son asylum, and make him
a sumptuous temple [...]; this king will always make you
fecund, the gods will protect you, and though your soil
be not fertile, strangers will bring you sacrifices whose
smoke will rise to the heavens."
(Latona addressing the island of Delos
when seeking refuge there.)

Homer, *Hymn to Apollo*

An ode to royal glory and the magnificence of the arts, Versailles offers its visitors a sumptuous decor. What would this manifestation of power and grandeur be, however, without the machinery that keeps it running, a link between great historical events and the less spectacular history of daily life? Under its ceremonial regalia, a little-known Versailles has many secrets to tell, in the heart of the city, in the corridors of the palace, and on the edges of the grounds...Opening a door or walking along a forgotten corridor is like going back in time to glimpse private moments that escape anyone in a hurry.

That's because Versailles—starting with the royal residence, of course, but including its extensions on the city and park sides—cannot be described by tour guides alone, no matter how knowledgeable they may be. History only reveals what it has seen fit to retain and invites visitors to play detective. If the meanings of things and places are not always apparent at first glance, they become strikingly clear a few steps further along. The palace, which Charles Perrault likened to a city unto itself, "superb in its grandeur, superb in its substance,"[1] links us to all those, illustrious or unknown, who once occupied it or walked through its hallways and reception rooms, giving us the chance to discern the spirits of the successive generations whose imprints seem to live on here. The interpretation of signs, especially when they relate to private spaces, is far from being an exact science. There are as many Versailles as there are viewpoints, and each era chooses the legends and characteristics it wishes to celebrate, depending on its own concerns, dreams, or failings. That leaves the visible—tangible objects... which rarely lie.

As they step into the secret recesses of Versailles, readers become privileged visitors, not only entering places normally closed to the public, but also gaining understanding of countless figures making up the "dream of kings." They can then gauge the scope of this complex organism playing on light and shade, exhibition and retreat, dedicated to the necessities of the practical exercise of power as well as the celebration of royal rituals, but also the preservation of privacy, always relative and temporary, of the king and his loved ones.

1. Charles Perrault, *The Century of Louis the Great*, 1687.

# BIBLIOGRAPHY

- Baraton (Alain) and Coffe (Jean-Pierre), *La Véritable histoire des jardins de Versailles*, Paris, Plon, 2007.
- Caffin-Carcy (Odile) and Villard (Jacques), *Versailles, le château, la ville, ses monuments*, Paris, Picard, 1991.
- Cornette (Joël), *Histoire de la France. Absolutisme et Lumières, 1652–1783*, Paris, Hachette, 2000.
- Da Vinha (Mathieu), *Le Versailles de Louis XIV, le fonctionnement d'une résidence royale au 17ᵉ siècle*, Paris, Perrin, 2009.
- Elias (Norbert), *La Société de cour*, Paris, Flammarion, "Champs" coll., 1985.
- Hours (Bernard), *Louis XV et sa cour*, Paris, PUF, 2002.
- Lemoine (Pierre), *Château de Versailles, guide du musée et domaine national de Versailles et Trianon*, Paris, RMN, 2002.
- Newton (William Ritchey), *Derrière la façade, vivre au château de Versailles au 18ᵉ siècle*, Paris, Perrin, 2008.
- Pérouse de Montclos (Jean-Marie), *Versailles*, Paris, Mengès, 1996.
- Solnon (Jean-François), *Histoire de Versailles*, Paris, Le Rocher, 1997, Paris, Perrin, "Tempus" coll., 2003.
- Tiberghien (Frédéric), *Versailles, le chantier de Louis XIV, 1662–1715*, Paris, Perrin, 2002.
- Verlet (Pierre), *Le Château de Versailles*, Paris, Fayard, 1992.
- Villard (Jacques), *Versailles, histoires et anecdotes en ville*, Bar-le-Duc, SPI, 2002.

## AND ALSO

- Bar (Virginie), *Dictionnaire iconologique, les allégories et les symboles de Cesare Ripa et Jean Baudoin*, Dijon, Faton, 1999.
- *Manière de montrer les jardins de Versailles par Louis XIV*, Paris, RMN, 1992.
- Ovid, *Les Métamorphoses*, French translation by Joseph Chamonard, Paris, Flammarion, 1993.
- Plutarch, *Vies parallèles*, French translation by Robert Flacelière and Émile Chambry, Paris, Robert Laffont, "Bouquins" coll., 2 volumes, 2001.
- Saint-Simon (Louis de Rouvroy, Duke of), *Mémoires, anthologie*, edited by François Raviez, Paris, Librairie Générale Française, "La Pochothèque" coll., 2007.

## MULTIMEDIA RESOURCES

www.sculpturesversailles.fr: "Versailles décor sculpté extérieur" by Béatrix Saule, head curator of the Palace of Versailles, and the RMN.

# COPYRIGHTS

**Editor** Laurence Solnais and Mathilde Kressmann
**Artistic Director** Isabelle Chemin
**Layout** Marylène Lhenri
With the collaboration de Anne Thomas-Belli, Laurence Alvado, and Julie Hiet

**Published in partnership with the public establishment of the Palace, Museum, and National Domain of Versailles.**
Jean-Vincent Bacquart, editor-in-chief, assisted by Anne Déon, Émilie Jacques, Corinne Thépaut-Cabasset and Cécile Bouchayer, with the collaboration of photographers Jean-Marc Manaï, Christian Milet and Christophe Fouin.

Printed in October 2018 on the presses of SEPEC in Peronnas (France)

**ISBN** 978-2-84096-751-4
**Dépôt légal** juillet 2011

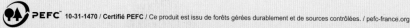

# VERSAILLES
# THE CITY

# THE MEASURE OF
# THE NEW CITY

**NOTRE-DAME CHURCH**
35, RUE DE LA PAROISSE

The entranceway of Notre-Dame Church, built between 1684 and 1686, looks extremely heavy and squat, and would surely have been improved if the 38-meter-wide structure had been balanced with more height. Did the brilliant Jules Hardouin-Mansart make a mistake when determining the proportions of the most important church in the royal city by limiting himself to just one storey above the thick cornice?

He did nothing of the sort, naturally. The building simply complies with the maximum height restrictions imposed by Louis XIV for buildings in the New City ("Ville-Neuve" in French), which were later forgotten during the speculative movements of the 18th century. To preserve the vistas, it was not possible to raise Notre-Dame higher than the palace overlooking it from a small hill. Likewise, structures in the New City were not permitted to stand taller than the famous cornice whose height had been set in relation to those of the façades of the Marble Courtyard. The type of houses defined by Louis XIV thus limited building height to two storeys with mansard roofs.

# MODEL HOME

**\*\* PAVILLON DES SOURCES**
11, RUE CARNOT

This house is contemporary with the court's move to Versailles and the development of the New City.
It provided official lodgings for the water-gate controller and the attendant in charge of maintaining the fountains. Originally, there was a lead tank behind this building which served as a reservoir of drinking water. This water was distributed throughout the neighborhood by eleven fountains modeled on the two magnificent ones located at the start of the ramps in the palace forecourt. The water came from springs in the forests of Marly and Chesnay, certified by the Royal Academy of Sciences in 1682.
The Pavillon des Sources (literally, "House of the Springs") dating from 1683 is one of the first built according to the regulations set by Louis XIV for domestic architecture within the New City. The anachronistic survival of this house is due to the fact that the reservoir kept working for nearly two centuries. In 1866, speculation hardly affected the historic center anymore and after being abandoned, the building became a residential building like any other.
The plaque on the second floor nevertheless reminds us that its architecture is in keeping with the "king's decree." This tidy construction features a play of colors between the brick facing and the limestone. Not all the houses in the New City, however, were constructed in the same way. Many could only imitate the model, faking brick and stone with a coating made by blending plaster and lime colored with red ocher (to resemble brick) or yellow (to resemble stone).

# DANCE CARDS

**\*\* HÔTEL DE LA CHANCELLERIE, GARDEN SIDE**
CURRENTLY THE REGIONAL CONSERVATORY
FOR MUSIC, DANCE, AND DRAMATIC ARTS
24, RUE DE LA CHANCELLERIE

This town house built in 1672 was the official residence of the Chancellor of France, one of the leading Great Officers of the Crown. It holds memories of the tenure of Louis Phélypeaux, Count of Pontchartrain, Chancellor from 1699 to 1714, and the sumptuous parties his wife gave there. The carnival of 1700 in honor of the Dauphine, Duchess Marie-Adélaïde of Savoie, was one of the masked balls of Versailles which only wound down after "eight o'clock in the morning," inspiring the Duke of Saint-Simon to write that "there were so many parties in Versailles at the time that one was delighted to see Lent approaching"! This account contradicts the common belief that Versailles was a bedroom community in which socializing was limited to court life at the palace. Although the construction of the South and North Wings in the 1680s and 1690s made it possible for more courtiers to live on site, in 1700 many nobles still resided in town.

Versailles was a lively city. From the outset of the establishment of the New City, Louis XIV created this dynamic, declaring that he wished the market town of Versailles to be "as flourishing and popular as possible." The king granted many privileges, giving away large plots of land that he guaranteed would not be seized.

On the eve of the Revolution, the "capital" of the kingdom was home to 55,000 people, a far cry from the cosmopolitan center of Paris, which then had 600,000 inhabitants, but also utterly different from the little hamlet of 500 souls it had been under Louis XIII, where the only event was the cattle market arriving from Normandy!

# DRIVE ON, COACHMAN!

**COACH GALLERY**
GRANDE ÉCURIE (GREAT STABLES)
1, AVENUE ROCKEFELLER
INFORMATION AT THE PALACE OF VERSAILLES

When the Museum of French History was created at the Palace of Versailles, Louis-Philippe bought the historically significant carriages on the civil list and had them placed in the Petite Écurie (Small Stables). This is how Versailles came to boast the seven Berlin carriages from Napoleon's wedding, the carriage from Charles X's coronation, the Berlin carriage from the Duke of Bordeaux's baptism, the hearse for the Duke of Berry and Louis XVIII, as well as three eighteenth- and nineteenth-century sedan chairs, in addition to the one Louis-Philippe used to visit the worksite for his museum!

This ensemble is only a fraction of the former Petite Écurie collection, which was broken up and sold during the Revolution: no fewer than 2,000 carriages preserved over three successive reigns after Louis XIV!

Nevertheless, the carriage of Charles X—the only surviving carriage from a French king's coronation—is a rare piece. Started for Louis XVIII, it was completed for the coronation of the king in Reims on May 28, 1825. Its splendor certainly rivals that of the coronation carriages of the Ancien Régime. Also worth noting is that it is quite similar to the Berlin carriage, invented in Berlin in the 17th century, because it has suspension making it lighter, faster, and more comfortable. The miniature carriage belonging to the Dauphin, the first-born son of Louis XVI, is a simpler, smaller example of the type of Berlin carriages likely used by the court day to day. In fact, it is the only original element of the largest collection of carriages ever constituted by a court.

# CITY
# OF HORSES

**\*\*QUEEN'S STABLES**
CURRENT APPEALS COURT OF VERSAILLES – 5, RUE CARNOT
TEL: 01 39 49 67 89 - WWW.CA-VERSAILLES.JUSTICE.FR

Riding arena in the Grande Écurie.

Any reference to horses in Versailles immediately calls to mind the Grande and Petite Écuries built by Jules Hardouin-Mansart between 1679 and 1683 on the goosefoot-shaped Place d'Armes. The royal city nevertheless had many other stables, including the Écuries de la Reine on Rue Carnot. Built in 1672, they started out as the king's stables and then became those of Queen Maria Theresa of Austria after 1682. Until the end of the Ancien Régime, they remained the stables of the queens and dauphines. However, the queen's and king's stables only housed a fraction of the equine population of the royal city, because each member of the royal family had their own stables, as did noblemen owning town houses, and there were also private horse-owners and stable leasers.

The king's stables housed 600 horses under Louis XIV, but that number kept rising, reaching 2,300 on the eve of the Revolution: 1,300 riding horses in the Grande Écurie and nearly 1,000 carriage horses in the Petite Écurie. The modernity of the infrastructure and the expertise of the personnel (nearly 1,000 people!) earned Versailles a reputation which extended beyond Europe. Its prestigious dressage school, founded under Louis XIV, developed equestrian art performances on a level never before achieved, featuring the horses as much as their riders. The Grande Écurie lent its central riding arena to royal festivities for events which also involved theater and opera. The site still upholds that artistic vocation with the Academy of Equestrian Arts run by the equestrian theater figure Bartabas.

Performance hall in the Academy of Equestrian Arts (restored by Patrick Bouchain).

# SELECT
# FRENCH PRODUCE

**ENTRANCE TO THE KING'S KITCHEN GARDEN**
10, RUE DU MARÉCHAL-JOFFRE
TEL: 01 39 24 62 62 - WWW.POTAGER-DU-ROI.FR

n 1876, Louis Edmond Cougny's statue of Jean-Baptiste de La Quintinie was installed above the entrance to the former storeroom for the king's kitchen garden, in which fruits and vegetables were sorted and kept. The statue honors the creator of this nine-hectare domain, laid out between 1678 and 1683, which revolutionized the art of crop growing. To protect the plants from wind and to optimize exposure, sixteen central vegetable plots were created, framed by four raised terraces and, behind high walls, twenty-nine closed gardens sheltered espalier-pruned fruit trees (pear, peach, plum, fig). This system, along with the *sous chassis* (under-frame) and *sous cloche* (under-cloche) sheltered growing methods,

with the addition of lots of manure, made it possible to create microclimates which allowed accelerated ripening in all seasons. That meant the king's table could provide lettuce in January, figs in February, strawberries in March, and asparagus all year round! This novelty marked a change from the old aristocratic mentality which discredited products linked to working the soil. However, only the most beautiful products were served at court; sometimes a tiny portion of the harvest was kept and the rest given away to the needy through the hatch still visible at 2, Rue Hardy. The refinement of this "select early produce" inspired much royal enthusiasm, and Louis XIV ennobled La Quintinie in 1687.

# THE HUMBLE MONKS
## OF THE INVALIDES

**ENTRANCEWAY OF THE CHURCH OF THE RÉCOLLETS**
RUE DES RÉCOLLETS, AT THE CORNER OF RUE SAINT-JULIEN

The first stone of this church and of the Récollets convent was laid by Louis XIV on March 10, 1684. With this construction, architect Jules Hardouin-Mansart created the city's second religious building, which served the Old-Versailles neighborhood, replacing Saint-Julien Church, which was demolished to make way for the Grand Commun.

These days however, the great door is no more than part of the wall of the neighboring convent; the rest of the church is gone. After its conversion into a prison in 1793, the church fell into very poor condition. In 1796, a plan to cut a new street to extend Rue Saint-Julien up to Rue du Jeu-de-Paume led to the destruction of its nave. The project was abandoned, but on the street side, all that remained was the church's entranceway and part of its sculpted decoration: two angels censing a cross, which is now lost, and the arms on the pediment. But make no mistake—the decorative simplicity of the stonework was the mark of the Récollets ("Recollects" in English), a religious order related to the Franciscans whose mission was to preach the gospel through poverty. Serving as military chaplains and stretcher-bearers in the king's regiments since Henry IV, they were established in Versailles in 1670 by Louis XIV to officiate for the companies of his all-important Maison Militaire (elite royal officers, guards, and troops).

# HEADQUARTERS OF THE FOUNTAINEERS

**ENTRANCE TO THE WATERWORKS**
**\*\* INTERIOR OF THE WATER TOWER**
1 BIS, RUE ROBERT-DE-COTTE

At the rear of the North Ministers' Wing, there is a collection of buildings which were closely linked to the hydraulic supply of the gardens of Versailles. One large three-storey brick house could be mistaken for a residence, but in fact it housed a massive 1,200-cubic-meter tank which sat 13 meters high, supported by thirty stone pillars, hence its name: *château d'eau* (water tower). Its construction in 1684 followed the destruction of the reservoir in the Téthys Grotto once found at the

opening of the North Wing. It was fed by underground conduits from the storage basins of the Butte de Montbauron, east of the city.

When the fountains were in operation, it emptied in 41 minutes, and 39 minutes more were needed to fill it again. Although the tank was removed at the end of the 19th century, interesting vestiges still remain inside the building, particularly the huge pillars. At 1, Rue Robert-de-Cotte, you can read the inscription that continues to mark the entrance: *Service des eaux* (Waterworks).

On the right, at the entrance to Rue du Peintre-Lebrun, you can see a little single-storey corner house, which stands out because of the stone arcature surrounding the window on Rue Robert-de-Cotte, probably the remains of the entrance to a town house which stood here before the house was built in 1686. It was the official residence of master fountaineer Claude Denis, who was in charge of operating the fountains and inspecting the conduits. Meanwhile, François Francine, fountain engineer and general intendant, lived at 14, Rue Hoche, not far from Notre-Dame Church, just next to André Le Nôtre, who lived at N° 16 on the same street.

Both of these town houses are now gone.

# THE MINISTRY
## OF THE KING'S GLORY

**\*\* FORMER HÔTEL DE LA SURINTENDANCE DES BÂTIMENTS DU ROI
(SUPERINTENDENCE OF THE KING'S BUILDINGS)**
4-6, RUE DE L'INDÉPENDANCE-AMÉRICAINE

Did everything really happen in such a small town house? Jean-Baptiste Colbert, followed by François Michel Le Tellier de Louvois, the masterminds of the Superintendence of the King's Buildings, had a hand in everything, and had at their orders the King's First Architect and First Painter, intendants, controllers, building masters, thousands of clerks and tens of thousands of workers on the sites! The "superintendent and general organizer for the buildings, arts, tapestries, and factories of France" was a real minister of culture before such a post existed, holding considerable influence over the artistic and scientific life of the time. While this administration's prerogatives were vast, nothing about this building's appearance advertises this fact. This is surely because all the hard work was focused inside the walls, commissioned by Louis XIV. When Colbert asked the king, in 1672, if he wanted long or brief reports, he answered: "Long. Details about everything." The Hôtel de la Surintendance was a simple office where, surrounded by a handful of clerks, the superintendent spent his time producing reports. The 1701 move to N° 9 of the same street under Jules Hardouin-Mansart, holder of the title since 1699, only provided a little more space. This town house, which he had built in 1683 for the Duke of Mortemart, was no more prestigious. The austerity of the undertaking remained unchanged. When the Revolution broke out, the last superintendent, the Count of Angiviller, accused of misappropriating public funds, had to emigrate to Germany. His wife was forgotten and remained there without being troubled until her death in 1808.

# THE ROCOCO
## SMILE

** **WEDDING ROOM IN THE CITY HALL**
4, AVENUE DE PARIS
WWW.VERSAILLES.FR

The sumptuous woodwork of the wedding room is the only vestige of the former Hôtel de Conti, site of the first Versailles City Hall before Mayor Édouard Lefebvre had it rebuilt in 1899. It attests to the taste for Rococo—a term composed of the French *rocaille* (rockwork) and the Italian *barocco* (baroque)—which became popular in the early 18th century, a fantastical style whose lines and curlicues recall the spirals of shells or floral furls. Created under the direction of Robert de Cotte in 1723 for the Duke of Bourbon, Louis XV's First Minister after the Regency, this woodwork was produced six years earlier than the decors ordered by Louis XV for Queen Marie Leszczynska's bedroom in the palace, which nonetheless were considered the first of the style in Versailles. Although this style is often associated with the (Parisian) Regency, the links between Rococo and Versailles are longstanding. In the last year of Louis XIV's reign, many artists had already embarked on this path. Working with rounded shapes and joyful lines, André Charles Boulle, Jean Berain, and Claude III Audran had left more room for sensitivity and imagination. The new fashion broke from Louis XIV-style stiffness, replacing it with a new "smile-eliciting" spirit, putting more emphasis on pleasure than on the pious virtues, morality, and reason dear to the Great Century.

# WHERE JUPITER
# FURIOUS COMMANDS

**\*\* FORMER HÔTEL DES GENS D'ARMES DE LA GARDE DU ROI**
**(HOUSING THE MEN-AT-ARMS OF THE KING'S GUARD)**
6, AVENUE DE PARIS

This magnificent entrance door with its sculpted decoration teeming with military trophies, flower garlands, palm leaves and shells, is all that remains of the Hôtel des Gens d'Armes de la Garde du Roi, which Louis XV had ordered to be built around 1735 on Avenue de Paris. Pride of place is given to the motto of this elite corps placed under the authority of his Maison Militaire: *Quo jubet iratus Jupiter* ("Where Jupiter furious commands"). Exclusively at the king's service, these 200 guards and 10 officers, all of noble birth, were identifiable by their red uniforms with black trim. At the time, Versailles was a real garrison town. No fewer than 2,000 men were stationed there, composing 14 companies grouped into two main corps. The "inside-the-Louvre guards"—composed of four companies of bodyguards, one hundred ordinary Swiss Guards, Guards of the Gate, and Provost Guards—watched over the inside of the palace; the "outside-the-Louvre guards"—made up of two regiments of French and Swiss Guards, two companies of musketeers, mounted grenadier guards, and light cavalry, as well as the men-at-arms—were in charge of policing the royal city. Even in peacetime, nearly 55,000 men were spread over regiments throughout the kingdom. Such a deployment had a price: 40 to 50 % of the entire State budget was swallowed by maintaining the troops alone!

# SQUARE
## DIGS

Despite his love of hunting, around 1685 Louis XIV decided to sacrifice Louis XIII's Parc aux Cerfs (Deer Park), located south of the city. Having undertaken to use the site for housing necessary for the growing population, as for the foundation of the New City in 1671, he conceded land with building plots laid out on a grid. Around the crossroads formed by the intersection of Rue Royale and Rue d'Anjou, the king even created a market, although it took some time to become established. This was accomplished in 1736 when ambitious entrepreneurs Jean Bully and Charles Bruneteau lined the crossroads of the two streets with low masonry buildings. Capped with mansard roofs, this group of buildings was to house merchants' stalls, grouped into four specialties (Carré de la Boucherie, Carré aux Herbes, Carré à la Marée, and Carré à l'Avoine—respectively for meat, herbs, seafood, and oats). It was not a success. Saint-Louis fell victim to competition from the older Notre-Dame market, established in 1669.

The entrepreneurs then ceded the shacks to a Parisian wood merchant, Robinet de Grenon, who turned them into a hay market (only the Carré à l'Avoine kept its original name). However, it, too, fell into disrepair in 1755, and the market was finally turned into housing when the mansard roofs were raised. Oddly enough, changing the buildings' function saved them, whereas Notre-Dame market was replaced between 1841 and 1842 by the four modern covered markets built by architect Eugène Le Poittevin and still in use today.

# FROM SENTRY
## TO BAR

**\*\* THE GUET DU ROY**
**(KING'S LOOKOUT)**
CORNER OF RUE NEUVE-NOTRE-DAME AND RUE PÉTIGNY

While policing and law enforcement in the city of Versailles were handled under the Ancien Régime by the services of the bailiff—whose lovely town house, dubbed "of the bailiwick," is right next to the current Passage de la Geôle (antique dealers' district)—, security fell to the guard companies of the king's Maison Militaire. Run by two Swiss Guards sent from the Hôtel des Invalides, this little building was a sentry post of the type often found at the corners of main streets. Its construction in 1783 by Jean-François Heurtier, under the reign of Louis XVI, was ordered by the Prince of Poix, governor of Versailles. It was used to watch over the wasteland of the former Clagny marsh, which was drained in 1736 after a severe episode of "paludian fever." This space in flux (delineated by the Boulevard du Roi, Rue Neuve-Notre-Dame, Rue Berthier and Rue du Maréchal-Foch near the Rive-Droite station) attracted a shady population, disliked by neighbors who were much more select and involved in the area's residential development.

The structure became national property during the Revolution, was sold to a horse trader from Tarbes, then changed hands a few more times before being turned into an *estaminet* (small bar) and taking on the name familiar to us today. This change of activity is less unusual than it might seem when you realize the Swiss Guards enjoyed the singular privilege of being allowed to bring wine into the city and sell it without having to pay a toll to Versailles. So, people went to the sentry post as you'd go to a tavern! It's unclear whether this helped public safety...

# MYSTERIOUS
## DOMES

**SAINT-LOUIS CATHEDRAL**
PLACE SAINT-LOUIS
TEL: 01 39 50 40 65 - WWW.CATHEDRALE-VERSAILLES.ORG

In 1743, Louis XV entrusted Jacques Hardouin-Mansart de Sagonne, grandson of Jules Hardouin-Mansart and great-nephew of Robert de Cotte, with the construction of the church for the city's new southern district. This church became a cathedral in 1790. Its two bell towers are an original shape, according to the canons of classical architecture, topped with four-sectioned domes capped with bulbous spires. This architectural theme recurs in the large dome at the middle intersection of the transept and the top of the Chapel of the Virgin. In this style redolent of the bell towers of northern Baroque architecture, some see a reflection of Gallicanism affirming autonomy from the Pope. Others detect the paying of homage to Queen Marie in an echo of the bell towers of her native Poland. In 1755, Louis XV did give the queen a gift of six bells, of which

the queen, the dauphine, and her four daughters (Adélaïde, Victoire, Sophie and Louise) were the patrons.

The use of onion-shaped domes, developed in the church of Saint Agnes in Agony in Rome by Borromini in the mid-18th century, was however not unheard of in Versailles. The Royal Chapel of the palace had a bulbous central lantern which was removed in 1765 because the roof was subsiding. Furthermore, the choice of this shape was not unrelated to the difficulties presented by the site—the spongy ground made it necessary, in building Saint-Louis Cathedral, to support it with posts and a vast stone foundation, with the consequence of having nave roofs less pitched than usual at the time. The onion-shaped domes would have been selected to cut down on weight without reducing the visual effect of height.

# SWEET WATERS
## OF VERSAILLES

On Place Saint-Louis stands a remarkable monumental fountain by Hubert Pluyette decorated with an elegant bas-relief depicting swans, dogs, rushes, and the mask of a triton. The inscription carved on it in 1856 evokes the efforts made by Louis XV and Louis XVI to supply "good drinking water" to the people of Versailles. Erected in 1766 by the building controller, engineer, and architect Hubert Pluyette, this fountain was part of a vast

undertaking to equip the new Saint-Louis neighborhood which did not have access to the water from the Pavillon des Sources in the Notre-Dame neighborhood. It was connected to a nearby reservoir in the Carré à la Fontaine, which was itself connected by underground conduits to the Butte de Picardie reservoir, in turn fed by Louis XIV's Marly Machine. The consumption of water from the Seine River downstream from Paris was not yet discouraged, and Louis XV even had some brought to him regularly. However, in the early 1780s, Versailles residents found Seine water revolting and learned men started accusing it of spreading diseases. Louis XVI then came up with a new project to clean it. In 1787, a process was adopted which involved filtering the water before it entered the Picardie basin, using two rows of four vats installed in what was named the "Pavillon des Filtres" (on what is now Avenue des États-Unis). Filled with different kinds of sand, these vats were supposed to trap microparticles and bacteria. Although it was no longer Seine water but rather well water from Croissy-sur-Seine which supplied Versailles from 1896 on, the Pavillon des Filtres and the Butte de Picardie reservoir continued operating until... 1964!

"Rushing water calls to you here,
It flows at the sound of the pastor's voice,
To quench all the thirsts of the heart
And wash stains from the soul."
(Translation of the inscription engraved on the Saint-Louis fountain.)

# SECRET RENDEZ-VOUS

**CORNER DOOR**
CARRÉ À LA TERRE

I n the early 1750s, the relationship between Louis XV and Madame de Pompadour turned into a platonic friendship. However, as rumor had it, to maintain her hold over the king, his former mistress would organize romantic encounters in the place called "Deer Park." People said that pretty young girls of low birth jostled for position in this luxurious place of ill repute. We don't know the exact location of this park, sometimes said to be at N° 82 Rue d'Anjou, sometimes at N° 4 Rue Saint-Médéric, and sometimes behind a wooden corner in the Carré à la Terre... The setting for these royal orgies was also said to have been the Ermitage (Retreat) of the Marquise, located beyond the Neptune Fountain. As criticism is born of jealousy, it's clear that Louis XV's 1749 decision to set aside no less than 6 hectares from the Petit Parc (Small Park) of the Palace of Versailles for Madame de Pompadour didn't go unnoticed. Between presents and acquisitions—the Château de La Celle, the Château de Bellevue, the Hôtel d'Évreux (currently the Élysée Palace where the French President resides)...—, the extremely preferential

treatment of the Marquise caused a scandal. The king let people talk. He already had a lot to handle on the political side: peace that brought no benefit after a costly war, difficult tax levying, and a parliamentary revolt. In that delicate context, a dark legend sprang from a disturbing sex case involving the kidnapping of children of Parisian artisans, finally triggering a crisis of confidence which came to a head on January 5, 1757 when a certain Robert François Damiens made a knife attack against Louis XV in the royal courtyard of the palace. So, legends and historical truths entwined over the course of the dark hours of the reign which saw the emergence of public opinion.

**Ermitage of Madame de Pompadour, 10, Rue de l'Ermitage, architect: Jean Cailleteau, a.k.a. Lassurance.

# THE ARMS
# OF THE MARQUISE

**\*\*FORMER HOUSE OF MADAME DE POMPADOUR**
7, RUE DES RÉSERVOIRS

At the end of the North Wing of the palace, below the big reservoirs of the Royal Opera, stands Madame de Pompadour's former town house, built in 1752 by her official architect Jean Cailleteau. At the outset, the main street-side façade only had one upper floor with a mansard roof. Yet the pediment of the fifth floor displays a Rococo blazon with the arms of the Marquisate de Pompadour with which Louis XV had ennobled his one-time mistress. What is such a blazon doing on a floor that didn't exist in the 18th century? Sold in 1794 as national property, the town house was purchased by a textile merchant who rented it to an innkeeper/caterer. In 1875, his successor turned it into a luxury tourist hotel under the name Grand Hôtel des Réservoirs, having expanded it by adding an attic floor to replace the former roof space. Then, between 1906 and 1907, two more floors were simultaneously added. The hotel catered to a prestigious clientele: politicians and diplomats of the Third Republic (which had its seat at the Palace of Versailles between 1871 and 1879), foreign guests like the Prince of Wales (the future Edward VII), prominent artistic figures from Parisian Belle Époque society, such as Marcel Proust, Henri de Régnier, Reynaldo Hahn, and Émile Zola.

Aware that the Marquise de Pompadour was the best possible ambassador for his illustrious establishment, the owner made sure her coat of arms was given pride of place. However, no one knows if it this coat of arms was salvaged from the original edifice or if it was created later.

# THE HARSH WORLD OF FINANCE

**\*\*FORMER HÔTEL DU GRAND CONTRÔLE
(TAX INSPECTION BUILDING)**
12, RUE DE L'INDÉPENDANCE-AMÉRICAINE

During the speculative adventure of John Law's Bank and the Mississippi Company, a certain Lady Chaumont, who had acquired an immense fortune by speculating on paper money, purchased this 1680s town house from the heirs of the Duke of Beauvilliers, Colbert's son-in-law. She was ruined by the bankruptcy of March 24, 1720 and had to sell her town house.

In 1724, Louis XV bought it and set it up as premises for the Controller General. Philibert Orry, who was at the head of this body between 1730 and 1745, was its wisest manager, even succeeding in 1739 and 1740 in having a slight surplus in the State budget. These golden years of the reign are a contrast, however, with the later downhill slide: just before the convocation of the States General by Louis XVI, debt repayment absorbed 42 % of the State budget. Between 1745 and 1789, there was a succession of no fewer than twenty different controllers in charge of finance.

One of them, Étienne de Silhouette, only remained Controller for nine months, although his name went down in history through the expression *à la silhouette*, referring to something with an unfinished aspect. Like his predecessors, Silhouette tried to tax the well-off, but his proposal to tax the external signs of riches—a tax on doors and windows—set him apart and made him unpopular.

# SAFE FROM
## FIRE

**ENTRANCEWAY OF THE FORMER HÔTEL DE LA GUERRE
(WAR BUILDING)**
3, RUE DE L'INDÉPENDANCE-AMÉRICAINE

This monumental entranceway topped with a royal crown and war trophies, with its radiant sun framed by pilasters adorned with military attributes, hides one of the most remarkable technical innovations of Louis XV's time. In 1758, it was with a view to limiting trips between Paris and Versailles that engineer and geographer for the king's armies Jean-Baptiste Berthier suggested building a *hôtel* devoted to the Secretary of State for War on the site of the Louis XIII's former kitchen garden. This structure would gather all the archives in one place. However, people were afraid of the risk of fire—the blaze which had devastated the Grandes Écuries in 1751 was still a vivid memory. So, the engineer proposed to make an inflammable building. Louis XV was reluctant. Nonetheless, open to scientific experimentation, he finally gave his consent. The six-storey building, constructed between 1759 and 1760, used no wood but rather thick brick walls, tile floors, and flat lowered brick vaults reinforced with iron tie beams. On June 26, 1762, before the archives had been transferred, Louis XV, accompanied by the Dauphin, came to inspect the building. Without consulting them, Berthier had bales of hay set on fire; there was no need to call the palace's "fountaineer firemen," because the fire didn't spread to the other rooms! The king was said to be very satisfied.

# TIME FOR REVENGE

**\*\* GALLERY OF THE HÔTEL DE LA MARINE ET DES AFFAIRES ÉTRANGÈRES (NAVY AND FOREIGN AFFAIRS BUILDING)**

CURRENT MUNICIPAL LIBRARY
5, RUE DE L'INDÉPENDANCE-AMÉRICAINE – TEL: 01 39 07 13 20
WWW.BIBLIOTHEQUES.VERSAILLES.FR

The Hôtel de la Marine et des Affaires Étrangères, built after the neighboring Hôtel de la Guerre, is famous for its grand gallery with its enfilade of seven rooms, which has retained its prestigious decor. Expressing the influence of France in Europe, the paintings by Jean-Jacques Bachelier and twelve lintels by Louis-Nicolas Van Blarenberghe depict the Vatican and Saint Peter's in Rome, Warsaw, Turin, Genoa, Berlin, Vienna, Naples, Madrid, London, Lisbon, Constantinople, and Parma. In the middle of the central room there was originally a marble table which was used during meetings of ambassadors, notably when treaties were being signed. As the Seven Years' War had shifted the center of military operations in Europe to the seas and the colonies, it's not surprising that this *hôtel* was chosen for this function by the Duke of Choiseul. Its decor signified it was time for revenge on the English who, during the peace treaty signed in Paris in 1763, had acquired almost all the French colonial empire. On May 15, 1768, the treaty which annexed Corsica to France was signed on that table. On September 3, 1783, it was the treaty by which England recognized the independence of the United States of America. That famous table has disappeared, as have the Foreign Affairs archive boxes which were organized by geographical section, now replaced by antique books. And what books they are! This priceless collection was gathered following the 1793 revolutionary confiscations from the libraries of aristocrats who had fled Versailles.

# THE KINGDOM
# GATHERS SPEED

**\*\* FORMER HÔTEL DES POSTES**
4, RUE SAINT-JULIEN

While we know that Louis XIV used the postal service to keep an eye on what the courtiers thought of him, we forget that it was also, and above all, used to develop a centralized administration. The Hôtel de la Poste aux Lettres which Louis XV had constructed in 1752 by Jacques Ange Gabriel in the ministry district was to facilitate the management of the correspondence and orders sent by the king. The *poste* (from the Italian *posta*) also referred to the place set aside in the stables of a posthouse for each horse carrying travelers and mail. Of the double doors called *entre-sort* (enter-exit), making it easier for riders to come and go, only the right door remains; the left has been walled up. These administrative stables were the core of a centralized postal and road network whose development was the great undertaking of

the 18th century. In less than half a century, the road and bridge engineers created more than 30,000 kilometers of pebbled roads, dotted with 1,320 posthouses! The result was that, on the eve of the Revolution, carriage speed had doubled, and all the major cities of the kingdom were less than twelve days from Versailles, a real revolution which stimulated exchanges and brought people and territories closer together.

This progress only benefited the rich and the king's officers, however: the five-day trip between Paris and Bordeaux in a *turgotine*, a modernized version of the Berlin carriage developed in 1775 at the request of Minister Turgot, cost 125 *livres* or pounds, the equivalent of a year's pay for an artisan. For a fifteen-day trip in the lowest class, in a *fourgon* (mail wagon), you had to pay no less than 50 *livres*!

# THE COUNTESS
# LIVES THE HIGH LIFE

**\*\* FORMER TOWN HOUSE OF GEORGES-RENÉ BINET, GARDEN SIDE**

CURRENTLY THE CHAMBER OF COMMERCE AND INDUSTRY
OF VERSAILLES VAL D'OISE-YVELINES – 21, AVENUE DE PARIS

This town house "between courtyard and garden" was built in 1751 for the Dauphin's first Valet de Chambre, Georges-René Binet. The Binets were an ennobled family who, already under the reign of Louis XIV, passed down the duty of acting as Garçons de la Chambre du Roi (servants of the king's bedchamber) for the Bourbons. Georges-René benefited the most from his duties: at the time of his death in 1761, his fortune was a little over one million *livres* and included numerous properties...

Entrance to the stables created by Claude Nicolas Ledoux for Countess du Barry.

This gives you an idea of the social position of certain servants in Versailles under the Ancien Régime.

In 1771, when Countess du Barry, Louis XV's last mistress, acquired the town house, it wasn't for her own personal use, but to house her domestic staff. Finding it too small for her requirements, she ordered extravagant stables from her protégé, architect Claude Nicolas Ledoux. She didn't have time to see the end result, because, after Louis XV's death in 1774, she had to leave Versailles, ordered by sealed letter to the Convent of Pont-aux-Dames in Meaux. The Count of Provence, brother of Louis XVI, bought the town house in order to house some of his servants. The stables, now belonging to Monsieur, were completed by Jean-François Chalgrin around 1780. The tympanum of the monumental doorway bears his arms. As for the Countess who retired to her Château de Louveciennes in 1777, she continued to live the high life before the revolutionary Terror was the end of her: she was guillotined on December 8, 1793.

# RETURN
## TO CLASSICISM

**CATECHISM OR PROVIDENCE CHAPEL
ADJACENT TO SAINT-LOUIS CATHEDRAL**
PLACE SAINT-LOUIS

We associate the birth of neoclassicism in Versailles with the patronage of Louis XV's mistresses Madame de Pompadour and Madame du Barry, as well as with the work of Jacques Ange Gabriel, the king's First Architect. But it was Louis-François Trouard, architect of the Academy of France in Rome who was the first to steer Versailles away from Rococo. The "charnel house" chapel, built in 1764, marked a return to streamlined decoration inspired by classical art. Intended to house the remains of members of the royal family, it only acquired its current name after the Revolution. With its Ionic columns supporting a little coffered dome in four sections, the building has no superfluous ornamentation. Its central "Roman-style" altar, placed as it would be in an atrium, bears a resemblance to the ruined villas of Herculaneum and Pompeii, engravings of which were circulating among architects and feeding their imaginations.

In the following years, Trouard continued in the same vein with Saint-Symphorien Church in Versailles, commissioned by Louis XV. Here again is monumental architecture inspired by classical art: a basilica floor plan, Tuscan fluted columns, a simplified decor and, above all, a plain coffered ceiling, which was completely unheard of in France at the time. The time of curves and counter-curves had passed; the king had had enough of them. It was time for clarity, geometry, and finely drawn lines, in the spirit of the Enlightenment.

# THE QUEEN'S
## WISHFUL THINKING

**\*\* ENTRANCEWAY OF THE CHAPEL OF THE AUGUSTINES
(OR THE QUEEN'S CONVENT)**
ACTUEL LYCÉE HOCHE – 73, AVENUE DE SAINT-CLOUD
TÉL. 01 30 84 08 50
WWW.LYC-HOCHE-VERSAILLES.AC-VERSAILLES.FR

In 1766, Queen Marie Leszczynska created a school for young women modeled on the Royal House of Saint-Louis in Saint-Cyr, which had fallen into disrepair. She placed the convent under the supervision of the canonesses of Saint-Augustin, having obtained Louis XV's permission to build on the site of the old Château de Clagny in Versailles and to use its stones. She didn't have the opportunity to admire her work, however, because she passed away on June 24, 1768. Her daughters Adélaïde, Sophie, and Victoire took charge of the worksite, assisted by their father. Although the king's attention soon strayed from this pious duty of remembrance, in the royal family, devotion was in the air; in 1770, the youngest, Madame Louise, took her vows at the Carmel de Saint-Denis to try to bring about her father's salvation. During the inauguration of the Queen's Convent on September 29, 1772, the king came to realize the extent of this when he saw the neoclassical bas-relief of the entrance to the chapel—it depicted Marie Leszczynska explaining to her daughters the reasons for the creation of this school. Louis XV nevertheless gave little thought to the criticisms some expressed over his sexagenarian passions...

As for the architect, Richard Mique, the magnificent chapel, inspired by Palladio's Villa Rotonda, propelled him to the top, to the detriment of the King's First Architect, Jacques Ange Gabriel. In 1775, Louis XVI bestowed that title upon Mique, who became Marie-Antoinette's official architect.

# THE PHILANTHROPIST KING

**\*\* CHAPEL OF THE ROYAL HOSPITAL OF VERSAILLES, FORMERLY RICHAUD HOSPITAL**
78, BOULEVARD DE LA REINE

The chapel of the former Richaud Hospital is a circular building that proudly bears references to the dome of the Pantheon in Rome and Bramante's Tempietto; it's also one of the most beautiful creations from the reign of Louis XVI, who commissioned Charles-François d'Arnaudin to build it in 1779. Taking an active interest in the project, the king wanted to supervise the plans for new royal hospital himself, asking that patients be given individual beds separated by curtains, as well as treatment by doctors who worked for the royal family. The chapel itself was designed as an ambulatory adjoining the patients' rooms so they could attend services on their rolling hospital beds. However, the history of this hospital truly began with Louis XIII, who turned an old leper house into an infirmary (on what is now Rue de la Paroisse). Subsequently, Louis XIV transferred the establishment to the current site; in 1670 he had ordered the construction of a much larger hospital placed under the authority of the nuns of Saint-Vincent-de-Paul. Jacques Ange Gabriel continued the work under Louis XV.

Louis XVI, the philanthropist king, doubled the establishment's endowment. Already in 1786 he had financed the Philanthropic Society of Paris' school for blind children, before granting it space in the building of the Grand Commun. The king was indeed driven by a certain ideal of charity, but what is such largesse in comparison to the millions of *livres* spent on the acquisition of the Château de Saint-Cloud and the Château de Rambouillet alone?

*Louis XVI Distributing Alms to the Poor of Versailles During the Winter of 1788* (1817), by Louis Hersent.

# VERSAILLES
# TREADS THE BOARDS

**\* INTERIOR, MONTANSIER THEATER**
13, RUE DES RÉSERVOIRS
TEL: 01 39 20 16 00 - WWW.THEATREMONTANSIER.COM

On November 18, 1777, with Louis XVI and Marie-Antoinette in attendance, 1,200 guests were present for the inauguration of the Grand Théâtre de Versailles, for which Joseph Aude's La Fête des Muses was performed. A sign that sociability was no longer the preserve of the aristocracy alone, this private theater was the first to be worthy of the name in Versailles. It all started in 1768 when former actress Marguerite Brunet, known as "La Montansier," was put in charge of running a humble little theater on Rue Satory in Versailles. In 1775, as she had acquired the favor of Marie-Antoinette and her reputation as a stage manager was solid, the king granted her the privilege of directing the performances, on the condition that she build a theater within two years. She then bought the plot of land from the king's First Valet de Chambre, Marc-Antoine Thierry de Ville-d'Avray, although it is unclear where she got the money for the transaction. The King's Architect and Inspector General of Buildings, Jean-François Heurtier, drew up the plans and entrusted the work to Pierre Boullet, theater inspector and machinist at the Menus-Plaisirs, while the decors were created by painter Pierre-Louis Bocquet.

The theater was so popular that people even flocked there from Paris. This success allowed La Montansier to go on to manage many other theaters in France.

She created a dozen Parisian performance halls, including the Théâtre des Variétés which she was still running in 1819, at the age of... 89!

# A LEARNED GARDENER'S
## LABORATORY

**ITALIAN MUSICIANS' HOUSE**
CURRENTLY THE MUSEUM AND HEADQUARTERS OF THE UNION
COMPAGNONNIQUE DU TOUR DE FRANCE DES DEVOIRS UNIS
15, RUE CHAMP-LAGARDE - TEL: 09 52 32 61 49
WWW.LECOMPAGNONNAGE.COM

Although we think of this ravishing structure in the then village of Montreuil near Versailles as being the one in which Louis XIV housed the Italian castrati Carli, Nardi, and Santoni during their visit in 1710, it dates largely from the mid-18th century. It was Madame d'Argenson, wife of Louis XV's Secretary of State for War, who in 1752 ordered the rebuilding of this house originally constructed between 1686 and 1692 for the musicians Joseph Chabanceau de La Barre and Antonio Bagnera (only the outbuildings still date from that time). However, as her husband had gone into exile in 1757 because of his hostility towards Madame de Pompadour, the property was purchased by the Countess of Marsan, Governess to the Royal Children.

The gardens, which are now public, have retained almost none of the experimental character intended when Louis-Guillaume Le Monnier created them in 1762. This botanist, a learned encylopedist and doctor to Louis XV, had distinguished himself along with Claude Richard in the acclimatization of rare species—he also trained his son Antoine in the King's Garden, in Paris. Le Monnier quickly earned the esteem of Louis XVI, who loved surrounding himself with men of science, and it is likely that he was called upon to replant the park, as well as to create the Queen's Grove in 1775. From his nursery in Montreuil, he supplied the royal family's properties. Named First Physician to the King in 1789, he accompanied the monarch to Paris right up until the latter's tragic demise. Upon his return to Montreuil, which Madame de Marsan was forced to leave when the Revolution broke out, he led the life of a recluse, devoting himself to writing. He died there in 1799, at the age of 92.

# THE GOOD LADY
## OF MONTREUIL

**\* MADAME ÉLISABETH'S ESTATE**
73 BIS, AVENUE DE PARIS
INFORMATION AVAILABLE AT THE TOURIST BUREAU
TEL: 01 39 07 78 78 - WWW.YVELINES.FR

After the Revolution, the Prince of Talleyrand is said to have declared: "Whoever has not lived in the years around 1780 has not known the pleasure of living." There was no place better than the village of Montreuil to illustrate this. With its ponds, springs, meadows, hedged farmland, and charming properties, it was a favorite destination for the ladies of the court, particularly the Princess of Guéméné. Becoming Governess to the Royal Children in 1776, she had a pleasure house built in the middle of vast grounds; she also had an English-style garden made by botanist Louis-Guillaume Le Monnier. The spendthrift Guéménés were saved from ruin by Louis XVI, who purchased the domain for his sister Madame Élisabeth; the nineteen-year-old didn't want to have to marry in order to stay at Versailles. Madame Élisabeth surrounded herself with close friends, particularly Madame de Mackau, her former governess, who lived on the property with her daughters. Charitable towards the local children and the sick, she became known as "the good lady of Montreuil" who convinced Louis XVI to join the village to Versailles in 1787. Although the house was transformed by the addition of two three-storey houses under the First Empire, and although, besides the orangery, most of the curiosities of the park (kitchen garden, dairy, and cowshed) have disappeared, the whole has nonetheless kept the bucolic nature celebrated by the poet Jacques Delille in his 1782 poem "Jardins" (Gardens) in 1782.

# ENGLISH WHIMSY

**\* PARC DE BALBI**
12, RUE DU MARÉCHAL-JOFFRE, NEXT TO THE KING'S KITCHEN GARDEN
INFORMATION AVAILABLE FROM THE VERSAILLES PARKS
AND GARDENS SERVICE - TEL: 01 30 97 82 30
WWW.VERSAILLES-TOURISME.COM

This little park was once the pleasure garden of the Count of Provence and his mistress, the Countess of Balbi. Undertaken in 1785, it has retained its lake as well as its rustic grotto tucked in the heart of a little artificial hill topped with a music pavilion which sets the scale of this miniaturized landscape. The watchwords here are sinuosity, irregularity, variety, and surprise, allowing visitors to rediscover the beauty of nature in a wild state.

This model originating from England around the 1750s, expresses the desire for freedom and dreams of exoticism characterizing this *fin de siècle*. The travel accounts introducing Europeans to the Chinese emperors' pleasure gardens—the famous *Description* by Jean-Baptiste Du Halde (1735) or the *Lettres édifiantes* (Edifying Letters) by the Jesuit brother Jean-Denis Attiret (1749)—, very popular during Louis XV's reign, had particularly fed the imagination of the new generation. Like the Asian *sharawadgi*, the art of these new gardens lay in the imitation of disorder and the randomness of nature. Enriched by the fashion for pastoralism, the technical was dressed up as "picturesque" (from the Italian *pittoresco*, which means "worthy of being painted") to produce veritable living tableaus very different from the ordered gardens of the time of Louis XIV. Perhaps the apparent rejection of codes and symmetry was not unrelated to the rumors of libertine practices which surrounded these gardens, particularly the Parc de Balbi?

# THE COUNTESS'
FOLLIES

**MADAME'S MUSIC PAVILION**
AVENUE CHAUCHARD, LEVEL WITH 111, AVENUE DE PARIS

Not far from Madame Élisabeth's estate can be found two follies which Madame, Marie-Joséphine of Savoie, Countess of Provence and sister-in-law of Louis XVI, had built on her property. She moved here in 1780 after purchasing it from the Prince of Montbarrey, who had been forced into exile because Marie-Antoinette disliked him.

Envious of the queen's domain at the Petit Trianon, the countess found this to be the ideal spot to let her imagination run wild. In 1784, she commissioned Jean-François Chalgrin to create an English garden with a lake, an artificial mountain, and several structures, as was the fashion: a Chinese pavilion, a belvedere, a little temple, thatched cottages, a dairy, and a music pavilion. Only the last two remain, as the park was sold after the Revolution and completely built up. The rustic dairy, set behind a classical temple portico made of

wood and bark, with a pediment and Ionic columns, is now inside a private residential park, while the remarkable music pavilion stands in the heart of Parc Chauchard. The pavilion's appearance has changed however, because two wings were added in 1820 by architect Jean-Marie Huvé at the request of the new owners, Louis XVIII's famous jewelers, Jean-Baptiste and François Mellerio. They were succeeded by the Prince of Mérode, then by Alfred Chauchard, co-founder of the Grands Magasins du Louvre in Paris. Unmarried and with no heirs, in 1902 he donated the park to the Société du Louvre so that it could build housing on it for employees of the Parisian store. He did however define one condition: that his statue on Avenue du Louvre be maintained in perpetuity.

** Madame's Dairy, 2, Rue Vauban,
architect: J-F Chalgrin.

# THE SITE
# OF THE LAST HURRAH

**OUTLINE OF THE FOUNDATIONS OF THE STATES-GENERAL ROOM**
HÔTEL DES MENUS-PLAISIRS,
CURRENT VERSAILLES CENTER FOR BAROQUE MUSIC
22, AVENUE DE PARIS
TEL: 01 39 20 78 10 - WWW.CMBV.FR

Nothing remains of the room where 1,200 deputies from the three orders (nobility, clergy and common people) gathered from all over France in 1789. On this occasion, their aim was to resolve the State's disastrous financial situation.

The outline of the foundations was recreated to commemorate the room following its destruction in 1801. The only thing that has survived is the grand staircase in the east wing, leading to the library of the Center for Baroque Music, which once served as meeting rooms for the clergy and nobility. This room nevertheless seemed destined to a fleeting existence right from the start. Before gathering the States-General, Louis XVI twice convoked assemblies of prominent figures, between 1787 and 1788. A room was improvised for this purpose using wooden panels from the "roving palace" the queen had ordered for the previous carnival ball. Its more monumental successor was created by the architects of the Menus-Plaisirs who were in charge of making the theaters and decors for royal celebrations. However, unlike the large neoclassical basilica featured in the famous engraving, the room designed by Pierre-Adrien Pâris was small and the deputies had to squeeze in. Only the king and queen were at ease, with their thrones on a majestic dais. In this artificial decor, history saw the abolition of privileges and feudalism on the night of August 4, and the adoption of the Declaration of the Rights of Man and of the Citizen on August 26. Louis XVI, who had convoked the first meeting of the States-General since 1614, played out the last major act of absolutism despite himself.

# THE REPUBLIC
## SETTLES IN

**\*\* DINING ROOM OF THE HÔTEL DE LA PRÉFECTURE ET DU DÉPARTEMENT**
11-13, AVENUE DE PARIS

Reprising the architectural cannons of the 18th century, the Versailles prefecture building was constructed by Édouard Charton between 1863 and 1867 on the site of Louis XIV's former kennels. It blends in so well with the heritage buildings in Versailles that you might almost forget it was built during the Second Empire. However, its rich history links it definitively with the destiny of the Third Republic. Following Napoleon III's defeat at Sedan on September 2, 1870, the city was taken over by the Prussian army laying siege to Paris.

On September 19, the Prussian king's army set up headquarters there, before moving in on October 5. It was from the Hall of Mirrors of the Palace of Versailles that the birth of the Second Reich was proclaimed by Kaiser Wilhelm I on January 18, 1871, ten days before the armistice, but the Prussians stayed until February.

On March 18, Adolphe Thiers, head of the executive, fled the rebellion in Paris and decided to take refuge in Versailles, where he was named "transitional" President of the Republic. He set up his apartments in the Hôtel de la Préfecture. In May 1873, it was Mac-Mahon's turn to be named President. While the parliamentarians remained undecided about the nature of the regime, the last Legitimist Bourbon pretender, Count of Chambord, grandson of Charles X, waited in vain for his return to power in a house located at N°5 Rue Saint-Louis. The republic, however, was here to stay, with its de facto institutionalization taking place in 1875.

Before the government and deputies returned to Paris in 1879, Jules Grévy, the first President of the Third Republic to be elected by parliamentarians, was the last illustrious guest of this house.

# THE PALACE

# WALKING
## THE BEAT

**ROWS OF PAVING STONES**
MAIN COURTYARD

I n the palace's first courtyard, there are six rows of paving stones which were used to guide the French Guards and Swiss Guards who had to present arms and sound the drums when an important figure arrived. Outside these grand occasions, they were posted in front of the main gate, preventing beggars, women of easy virtue, or individuals with smallpox from coming any closer. Although during the day the palace was open to anyone properly dressed, access to the royal family and the king was tightly controlled. The Provost Guards who acted as police kept watch, and whenever the king moved around, he was always surrounded by four bodyguards, so that he could only be seen from afar. The palace functioned like a series of increasingly policed airlocks as you got closer to the seat of power; this is illustrated by the architectural organization of increasingly small courtyards. To be admitted into court, you had to have a rock-solid network of well-placed friends and relations: no one could get in without an introduction and a sponsor; lesser nobility or rich members of the bourgeoisie would even be required to purchase a *brevet d'affaires* (allowing them access to the king while he did his business) or a document giving them the right to serve! Living court life to the full, participating in the famous apartment soirées or the "king's pleasures," was limited to a privileged few. Courtiers accorded access had to be able to maintain a certain lifestyle and a large staff, and wear ostentatious attire. They were expected to adopt the style of the court and the particular civility of the well-born to be admitted to "that country" where honors were taken seriously.

# MY FATHER'S GLORY

## GLORY

**MARBLE COURTYARD**

Louis XIV was determined to preserve the palace of his childhood, the one his father had ordered to be built between 1631 and 1634 by Philibert Le Roy. This building was unique for its red-brick and ochre-tinged limestone façade as well as its high slate roofs. However, the king gave it a monumental appearance which would have made it quite difficult for Louis XIII to recognize his little hunting palace.

Between 1661 and 1682, the three façades were gradually redesigned. The windows were heightened and many classical busts were installed. Numerous gilded lead ornaments were added to the roofs, the brick cladding was painted red, and the old central balcony on the second floor was turned into a portico with four double marble columns. The biggest change came during the third works campaign, which began in 1678. The main building was raised with the addition of an attic floor adorned with a sculpted ridge and a clock, while the number of windows along the façade grew from five to seven. A balustrade decorated with flame vases (formerly thought to be topped with fleur de lys) and groups of sculptures was also added along the roof, whose dormers were completely altered. Over twenty years of works, Louis XIV was painstakingly attentive in his constant alteration and reworking of the shape and style of his father's palace, building a genuine legend.

# STAIRCASE
# OF THE DUPES

**\*\* SPIRAL STAIRCASE**
PASSAGEWAY OPENING ONTO THE ŒIL-DE-BŒUF ROOM
QUEEN'S INNER ROOMS

A great deal has been said about this spiral staircase hidden behind a door. For example, it's been suggested that it was a secret passageway used by Marie-Antoinette to meet Axel Fersen, who was staying above her. And yet, it is nothing more than a servants' staircase like dozens of others at Versailles, used by domestics of the royal family every day.

When we look into the time at which it was built, the dark little passageway snaking through the thick palace walls is the oldest of them all. Some say that this staircase, which led to the upper floors at the southwestern corner of the original main building, dates back to Louis XIII's second palace, built between 1631 and 1634. Others say it was part of Louis XIV's first works campaign between 1661 and 1668. In any case, the name it is sometimes given—
"Staircase of the Dupes"—is not entirely appropriate because it is not contemporary with the infamous Day of the Dupes on November 10, 1630, when Louis XIII, against his mother Marie de'Medici's advice, reiterated his support for the Cardinal de Richelieu from his palace at Versailles. The anachronism of this spiral staircase, compared to the straight staircases which became the norm at Versailles under Louis XIV, is not enough to establish its primacy.

# ARTISTIC SPLENDOR
## AND SUFFERING

**DARIUS' FAMILY AT THE FEET OF ALEXANDER (1660), BY CHARLES LE BRUN**
MARS ROOM
KING'S GRAND APARTMENT

This painting depicts the favor Charles Le Brun enjoyed with the king, as well as his misfortune. Created in 1660 under the gaze of Louis XIV at the Palace of Fontainebleau, the painting won the 27-year-old king's admiration as he searched for a talent for his Palace of Versailles. A student of Nicolas Poussin, Le Brun had mostly worked on the prestigious decoration of the Palace of Vaux-le-Vicomte, property of Nicolas Fouquet. After the Superintendent of Finance fell into disgrace, Le Brun became director of the Royal Academy for Painting and Sculpture and First Painter to the King, achieving a spectacular ascension. From 1663 onwards, he was in charge of overseeing the creation of the Apollo Gallery in the Louvre. He was then given free rein at Versailles, where, for nearly twenty years, a series of projects was carried out at breakneck speed. Thanks to this œuvre, he is seen by historians as the greatest French painter of the 17th century. However, many of his contemporaries did not share this view. The Duke of Saint-Simon went so far as to claim that the vault of the Hall of Mirrors was not his work, but rather that of Pierre Mignard who succeeded Le Brun as First Painter to the King.

Deeply unpopular, one year before his death, the master was dealt the coup de grâce: Mignard presented Louis XIV with a replica of the painting *Darius' Family* which won the court's admiration.

# THE HEROES
# OF LOUIS-DIEUDONNÉ

**CLASSICAL BUSTS**
MARBLE COURTYARD

The trumeaus of the Marble Courtyard boast a wonderful collection of emperors and divinities: 84 busts set on consoles, some of which are said to be antique, others of which are said to be copies. Created in 1665, these highly symbolic busts give us an insight into Louis XIV's personality. The references to the heroes of antiquity—Cyrus, Demetrius, Julius Caesar, Augustus, Mark Antony, Titus, Alexander Severus, Constantine, Alexander the Great—as well as to the Greco-Roman pantheon go beyond the iconographic program Le Brun applied to the rest of the palace's decor to glorify the actions of Louis XIV. The genesis of their development can be found in Plutarch's *Lives of Illustrious Men*, a text focused on the biographies of Greek and Roman figures.

Le Brun thus depicted morals exalting the timeless values specific to great men in their heroic exercise of power. Each bust expresses a particular virtue. The figures were perfectly recognizable to people at the time because Plutarch was one of the most-read and pondered classical authors in the 18th century. The Roman writer also had great influence on Mazarin's political training of the young Louis XIV. After losing his father when he was five years old and enduring a difficult childhood during the Fronde, the king certainly found in this text the examples he needed to build his personality and his future renown. This is why as an adult he never forgot the virtues of these illustrious men who would forever remain in the imagination of that reign.

# FLIGHT
# OF THE EAGLE

**MARS AND HERCULES AT REST (1679, REWORKED IN 1869)**
TYMPANUM OF THE CROWN OF THE AVANT-CORPS
MARBLE COURTYARD

nitially, the allegorical group designed by Le Brun in 1678 depicted Mars and Hercules leaning on their military trophies with various animals at their feet. On the right, beside Mars, the lion and the eagle symbolized Spain and the Holy Empire defeated by Louis XIV during the Dutch War (1672–1679). On the left, beside Hercules, were the Achelous bull, a metamorphosed river against which he fought, and the Lernean Hydra, which he killed. The latter, less explicit figures, made reference to the same events, the hydra being the Great Alliance raised against France and the bull symbolizing Louis XIV's glorious crossing of the Rhine with his army on June 12, 1672. The bull, hydra, lion, and eagle thus retraced a history of conflict, from left to right.
The sun emblem leading the march of time

at the center of the clock face completed the presentation: from Hercules to Mars, the victorious Louis XIV moved from heroic demi-god status to God of War status. However in 1869, the sculpture group's deterioration led to a faulty reconstruction that stripped away the meaning of the allegory. The sculptors Chapu and Jacquemond substituted the lion-eagle pair with a ram-lion pair. As the new sculpture was created under the Second Empire, which had the eagle as its emblem, the sculptors must have deemed it wiser to make the original bird disappear. This was a transformation that ruined the originality of a misunderstood work: the first representation of the mythic saga of the Dutch War, nearly three years before Charles Le Brun undertook to depict it on the ceiling of the Hall of Mirrors.

# THE WORLD
# ACCORDING TO COLBERT

**AMERICA AND AFRICA** (1678–1679)
MARBLE COURTYARD

On the south façade of the Marble Courtyard, you can see two sculpted women sitting on the balustrade, one coiffed with an elephant mask and the other with feathers, a crocodile at her feet. These allegories of Africa and America are echoed on the north façade by Asia, with her turban and her pot of perfume, and Europe, with her helmet and baton of command. These statues are part of a vast decorative ensemble spreading all the way along the balustrade. The *Royal Virtues* are presented as fourteen figures of women, each holding her attribute: *Wisdom* is associated with Minerva's owl, expressing philosophy and intelligence, *Prudence* holds a mirror to remind us of the necessity of self-knowledge, *Glory* has her arm around a pyramid, a symbol of princely aura... Starting from the back of the courtyard, where Apollo's sun sits in the center of the clock,

the two allegorical axes leading to the Ministers' Wings describe the virtues of a certain policy: from left to right, we see the pairs *Renown* and *Victory*, *Glory* and *Peace*, *Authority* and *Diligence*, *Wealth* and *Prudence*, *Generosity* and *Wisdom*, *Strength* and *Justice*, *Abundance* and *Magnificence*. This interplay of correspondences developed by Le Brun and based on Cesare Ripa's collection of allegories, *Iconologia*, illustrates Louis XIV's grand political design, orchestrated from the 1660s onwards and embodied by Colbertism, which led to administrative reform and encouraged domestic and colonial trade. For the elite, mythology was a key to the world, and the king's contemporaries accordingly perceived it as a symbol of his universal glory and a manifesto of his power over men and civilization.

# AN AIR
# OF TUSCANY

## ** VESTIGE OF THE WALL OF THE FORMER TERRACE
### ATTIC SPACE ABOVE THE HALL OF MIRRORS

I n 1668, Louis XIV decided to double the surface area of his father's old palace and asked Le Vau to build a U-shaped wraparound on the garden side. In the center, it was decided there would be a marble-paved terrace on the second floor, to create a lookout over the view of the Grand Canal. For a dozen years, this terrace separated the symmetrical apartments of the king and queen. At the time, Louis XIV's bedroom was a central room which cut the new palace in two.

Nonetheless, in 1677, when the king decided to set up permanent residence at Versailles, it seemed necessary to create a hallway linking the king's and queen's apartments: this would be the famous Hall of Mirrors, on the site of the terrace. The sculpted wall we see photographed here in the attic above it is the last visible remnant of the old façade. On the new one, on the eight spans on the

left and right, you can also make out traces of the removal of the terrace, which Jules Hardouin-Mansart attempted to minimize. Besides the ease of communication it offered, this renovation was also due to climatic reasons, as a palace resembling a pleasure villa was not suited to the harsh Île-de-France winters. Inside, the 357 mirrors installed in place of the French doors were not entirely capable of recreating the first palace's original effect of transparency between courtyard and garden.

View of the Palace of Versailles over the Water Parterre, around 1675, before the construction of the Hall of Mirrors.

# THE DISORDER
# OF THE PLANETS

**APOLLO DRIVING THE SUN'S CHARIOT (1671–1678), BY CHARLES DE LA FOSSE**
APOLLO ROOM
KING'S GRAND APARTMENT

In 1662, Louis XIV chose the sun as the "body" or image of his motto: *nec pluribus impar* (without equal). This was his way of marking his preeminence over his father-in-law, King Philip IV of Spain, who went by the description *el Rey Planeta* (the Planetary King). This symbolism is not unrelated to the Copernican revolution which made a great impression on seventeenth-century thinkers. After Copernicus proved that the planets orbited the sun, people realized that the universe was a vast machine ruled by physical laws. As the king represented God on Earth, his role was to administer and regulate the world.

At Versailles, the Apartment of the Planets, created by Le Brun, illustrates this turning point in scientific thought. Its seven rooms *en enfilade* correspond to the seven planets known at the time, which had been associated with gods since Ptolemy. The central room, under the auspices of Apollo to whom Jupiter was said to have entrusted the task of driving the Sun's chariot to bring light to the universe, introduced the following order in the apartment: Diana, Mars, Mercury, Apollo, Jupiter, Saturn, and Venus. However, when work began on the Hall of Mirrors and the War Room in 1681, this lovely celestial dynamic was shattered: the Jupiter, Saturn, and Venus rooms were destroyed and, in 1683, the Abundance Room was set up at the entrance of the apartment, while at the same time the Venus Room was repositioned before the Diana Room.

Meanwhile, the installation of the court had obliged Louis XIV to withdraw permanently to his new apartments over the Marble Courtyard.

# VERSAILLES
## PARQUET

As evidenced by the door frame between the Diana and Mars Rooms, the floors of the Grand Apartments were originally paved with marble. However, due to seepage of washing water and in the interests of comfort, the tiles were replaced by a new kind of parquet floor: "Versailles parquet," laid down in panels approximately one meter square, bordered by a framework of floorboards crossed like tilework. Put together like pieces of a big puzzle, this allowed large areas to be covered fast while the court retired, as every fall, to Fontainebleau, until the palace was back in order. Above all, this invention represents a break with the Italianate spirit of the first Versailles decors. The Apartment of the Planets was inspired, for example, by the decor of the *Sale degli Planetti* of the Palazzo Pitti in Florence, created around 1640 and which Le Brun had seen during his trip to Italy with Nicolas Poussin: Florentine marble on the floor and walls, vaulted painted ceilings with coffers decorated with Venetian-style sculpted stucco, built-in chimneys, *trompe-l'œil* canvas paintings... However, as his taste evolved and Colbert worked to use more French materials, Louis XIV began dreaming of a new, autonomous style. This is how the "French style" was born in the mid-1680s; marble surfacing was replaced by wooden floors and woodwork sculpted into floral shapes against a white background. In 1684, it was Jules Hardouin-Mansart who first had the idea of making pilasters not of marble but of gilded wood.

# THE AMBASSADORS'
## ENTRANCE

**\*BACK OF THE DOORS OF THE DIANA ROOM**
LANDING OF THE GREAT STAIRCASE (ESTABLISHED BY LOUIS-PHILIPPE)

Nothing remains of the Ambassadors' double staircase, destroyed in 1752, except the back of the panels of the doors to the Diana and Venus Rooms. Leading to the King's Grand Apartment since 1679, this ceremonial element of considerable size was virtually unique in France. To Louis XIV, it constituted a manifesto of his power as well as a means of intimidating foreign diplomats who sometimes pushed their mission over the line to brush with espionage.

On the ground floor, in the former vestibule of the staircase, a 1958 model depicts this luxurious display of power (photo above). Covered with polychrome marble, the staircase made an impression with its *trompe-l'œil* vault and its great rectangular wall of crystal mirrors rimmed with gilded metal which gave the impression of a much larger space on a par with the Baths of Caracalla in Rome. The rushing sounds of the triple cascade of water from the central fountain undoubtedly crowned the breathtaking effect of the whole. Visitors from around the world spread the word. Thus in 1712, Cardinal Alessandro Albani presented as a gift to Louis XIV *The Marine Centaur Abducting a Silenus*, a classical white marble statue (now in the Louvre) to add to the central fountain. The unfortunate demolition of the staircase ordered by Louis XV only served to amplify the myth. For example, a copy of the staircase can be found near Munich, in Herrenchiemsee Palace, which King Ludwig II of Bavaria intended to be a replica of Versailles.

# SUCH PANACHE!

**BUST OF LOUIS XIV (1665), BY LE BERNIN**
DIANA ROOM
KING'S GRAND APARTMENT

In 1665, these two busts of Louis XIV at the age of 27 were the fruit of a competition between two schools of sculpture represented by Jean Warin, champion of the French School, and Bernini, one of the geniuses of the Italian Baroque. While the first bust was lauded for its classical purity, the second was deemed too expressive. To many, this was proof that French art no longer needed to take lessons from anyone. However, it seems that Louis XIV quite liked the work by Bernini, whom he summoned to France—after putting pressure on Pope Alexander VII—to entrust him with the expansion of the Louvre. When he arrived in Paris, the master was treated with great honor. He took advantage of the time he spent with the king to capture the movement of his body, his panache, and his aura. Rather than imposing on Louis XIV by getting him to sit for him, Bernini followed the king around with a sketchbook. The resulting bust shows the king in profile, surging majestically from moving drapery. In comparison, Warin's work seems drawn

from a scholarly numismatic study, as was fitting for him, the controller and engraver-general of the mints of France.

Patriotism won the day, and in 1679 Warin's sculpture was put on display in the central niche of the Ambassadors' Staircase, while Louis XIV chose to put the Italian master's marble sculpture in the Diana Room. Ironically, the latter is still in place, but Warin's bust was moved by 1681 and more or less forgotten. In the Venus Room, however, you can see another one of his works, from 1668, depicting Louis XIV as an *imperator*... Its vitality seems to owe a debt to Bernini's influence.

*Bust of Louis XIV*, Eighteenth-Century Rooms, North Wing, by Jean Warin

# BEAUTIES
## OF THE COURT

**PORTRAITS OF WOMEN IN THE COURT OF LOUIS XIV**
SEVENTEENTH-CENTURY ROOMS
NORTH WING

Set high in a row in one of the music rooms of the North Wing, these eighteen portraits of women of the court of Louis XIV painted by Henri and Charles Beaubrun are enigmatic. They are all in profile and in the same rectangular format; they seem to have been intended to be part of the decor of a "room of beauties." There is however no trace of such a place or such an order in the archives, except for a request from painters addressed to Colbert in 1663. They wrote to the minister to complain about their financial difficulties, for under the Regency their talents were used less to magnify the women of the aristocracy. Standing out amid the beauties of the kingdom at Versailles were Duchess of La Vallière, Princess Henrietta of England, the Princess of Soubise, and the Princess of Monaco, whom people said was "cool as a sorbet." Although these portraits fail to capture each woman's individual beauty, their artifice betrays the women's condition, often forced to marry—this was the case of Anne Marie Martinozzi, who became the wife of the old Prince of Conti despite the fact she loved the Duke of Candolle—or doomed to end up in a convent. According to aristocratic tradition, love was of no consequence and youth was seen as a commodity. As Louis XIV himself had been obliged to forget his first love, Marie Mancini, he may have held some nostalgia for a time when State matters had not yet become all-important.

# THE KING'S
## HEART

**HYMEN'S TROPHY** (1681), BY BENOÎT MASSOU AND PIERRE LEGROS
LANDING OF THE QUEEN'S STAIRCASE

This trophy in *métail* (an alloy of pewter and copper) depicts two cherubs holding an escutcheon topped with two doves and the nuptial torches of Hymen, the Roman god of marriage. It refers to Louis XIV's marriage to his cousin Maria Theresa of Austria, an alliance designed by Mazarin to reconcile France and Spain. Sealing the peace treaty of the Pyrenees (1659), this marriage was a very political one, a fact which the king never allowed his queen to forget throughout her life. Before she died, Maria Theresa declared: "I have had but one happy day since I became queen." She had grown up knowing she would one day marry her cousin, and life at court had been full of disillusionment. Because her French was poor, she was quickly sidelined. At the end of her life, the queen could count on Madame de Maintenon, who worked to bring the spouses closer together. She remarked: "God led Madame de Maintenon to give the king's heart back to me!" After her death in 1683, she was quickly forgotten. The king took over her apartment, setting up Madame de Maintenon in it after their secret marriage. The Queen's Staircase then became the busiest in the palace, crowded with a crush of courtiers every day… No one paid any attention to the famous trophy created in 1681. The Revolution finished the job of removing any memory of the queen: Louis XIV and Maria Theresa's interlaced monograms, removed at that point in time, were replaced during the trophy's restoration by two entwined "L"s.

# THE FATE OF QUEENS
## WITHOUT REIGNS

**BAS-RELIEFS OF WARRIOR QUEENS (1671–1678)**
CEILING OF THE ANTECHAMBER OF THE GRAND COUVERT
QUEEN'S GRAND APARTMENT

Accompanying the painting in the center of the ceiling, a replica of Le Brun's *Darius' Family at the Feet of Alexander*, there are six magnificent bas-reliefs in simulated gold retracing the history of the heroic ancient queens who stood out by their bravery in battle: Harpalyce, Clelia, Artemis, Zenobia, Hypsicratea, and Rhodogune. Perhaps when Maria Theresa of Austria dined here in public with Louis XIV, she contemplated these scenes and thought about the subordinate role assigned to her by the court. Whatever the case may be, the warrior queens failed to bring the imperial princess any luck; she died at the age of 45 of a poorly treated benign tumor. From then on, her daughter-in-law, the Grande Dauphine Maria Anna Christina of Bavaria, took her place at the table. Her fragile health and plaintive nature however repulsed Louis XIV,

who left her to her taste for solitude, going into a neighboring room to dine. In 1690, the Grande Dauphine, too, died prematurely, at the age of 29. The Queen's Grand Apartment was closed for nearly twenty-one years, after the Grand Dauphin had retired to Meudon, officially marrying his mistress Marie-Émilie de Joly de Choin against his father's wishes. It was only in 1711, after the Grand Dauphin's death, that Marie-Adélaïde of Savoie, the new dauphine, took up residence in the Queen's Grand Apartment and brought Louis XIV back to it to dine. However, she was struck down the next year, at the age of 27, in a measles epidemic. The place was closed once again until the 1725 marriage of Louis XV and Maria Leszczynska, daughter of the dethroned king of Poland, who remained in the Grand Apartment for forty-three years!

# BABYLONIAN
## FEAST

**\* FIRST ANTERCHAMBER**
KING'S APARTMENT

The sober decor of this room shouldn't obscure the fact that Louis XIV invited an audience here every Saturday and Sunday night for theatrical presentations. Seated at a large rectangular table, surrounded by his children and grandchildren, he faced a crowd, among whom only duchesses were allowed to sit on folding chairs during the 45-minute Grand Couvert (dinner). Six paintings by Joseph Parrocel, ordered in 1686, set the tone, showing different classical battle scenes, particularly sieges. The aura of the warrior king is magnified here, as it would have been during the public meals Louis XIV liked to hold in cities fallen to victorious sieges. At Versailles, ceremony was extremely codified. First, the Officers of the Goblet presented the king with the "ship"—a silver object shaped like a dismasted ship which held his napkins—, before which everyone had to bow. Then an officer tasted the soft interior of the bread, after rubbing it on the plates to make sure there was no risk of poisoning, and the usher struck his baton of command, announcing: "Gentlemen, the king's meat!" Next the maître d'hôtel guided the long procession, protected by guards, of Officers of the Kitchen who presented a succession of dishes while musicians played Lalande's *Symphonies*. Behind the king stood the First Physician, two Officers of the Kitchen, the Captain of the Bodyguards, and the cupbearer in charge of serving drinks. Designed to impress, the scene was like observing a legendary meal of a classical hero to whom Louis XIV enjoyed being compared, like Alexander crowned King of Asia, feasting in Babylon.

# INSPIRED
# BY DEMOCRACY?

*ARISTOCRACY AND DEMOCRACY* (1681–1682)
CENTRAL AVANT-CORPS (2ND GROUP FROM THE LEFT)
SOUTH WING

Among the twelve pairs of allegorical statues installed in 1682 above the avant-corps of the South Wing, there is the strange union of *Aristocracy* and *Democracy*. The former is looking to her right, towards *State Interest*, recognizable by her plumed helmet. She is covered in drapery and wears a veil held in place by a wrought metal band. At her feet, there is a vase and coins which, according to Cesare Ripa's *Iconologia* show that "money is the sinews of war, and, if peoples want to keep it, they must not be stingy with it." Meanwhile, *Democracy* holds in her left hand snakes that "signify that the people usually have no consideration for true glory, as their government simply crawls"... an indication of its compatibility with Sun King absolutism!

It seems that after *Democracy*, Le Brun didn't really know which figures to place in the ranks of the *Forms and Virtues of Governance*, four pairs of which were meant to occupy the whole central avant-corps of the façade. In the end, he finally drew *Strength* and *Courage*, then, with no more logic, *Poetry and Music*. Although for a while he had thought to develop along the new South Wing an allegorical political theme comparable to the one running along the courtyards on the city side, he didn't take it any further. As allegorical representations were limited in number, to decorate the massive new South and North Wings, it became necessary to vary the attributes and genders of statues representing seasons, muses, and the arts.

# A NEW
# FRENCH ORDER
**HALL OF MIRRORS**

The decoration of the Hall of Mirrors carried out by Le Brun from 1681 to 1684 is a work of propaganda exalting national genius. Marble and mirrors—everything here is from France! The modern order featured on the capitals of the pilasters running along the mirrored walls was designed by Le Brun to represent the nation: to the leaves of the traditional Corinthian order were added Gallic roosters with a central figure of a fleur de lys crowned with a radiant sun. It was a reminder of who was ruler. The account of the civil and military works of Louis XIV, accomplished in under twenty years, runs for 73 meters along a nearly 1,000-square-meter vault. In 1685, the mottos accompanying these "learned images" celebrating this adventure were finally written in French, and not in Latin, by François Charpentier, Nicolas Boileau, and Jean Racine. Le Brun's pictural work was itself extraordinarily modern. After the triumphal return from Nijmegen in 1678, the glory of Louis the Great was unreservedly acclaimed, and the painter abandoned the planned Herculean metaphor to represent the king in person, making sure "not to include anything which was not truthful." Shown emblematically in the great central painting of the vault, *The King Governs by Himself*, Louis XIV appeared explicitly for the first time in the decor of Versailles without the mediation of myths, gods, or classical heroes.

# FOR ALL THE STATE'S GOLD

**CEILING OF THE ABUNDANCE ROOM**
KING'S GRAND APARTMENT

Around an ersatz sky, spread around the rim of a false cornice symbolizing the opposition between the sky and the ground, the soul and earthly riches, there are representations of precious objects which remind us of Louis XIV's taste for collecting. The central door of the room, above which there is the figure of Abundance and the royal ship, originally opened onto the king's Cabinets of Medals, Curiosities and Rarities, where Louis XIV showed a privileged few his most beautiful pieces.

The King's Grand Apartment also featured sumptuous silver furniture designed by Le Brun and created at the Gobelins factory by the team of silversmiths Claude Ballin and

Filippo Caffieri: tables, seats, mirror frames, chandeliers, candelabras, vases, caskets... and even a sumptuous solid silver throne. All of it was melted down in 1689 to pay for the war with the League of Augsburg. These priceless pieces of worked silver were in fact the materialization of the treasure which slept in State coffers. The Grand Apartment was a showcase for the royal factories, which Colbert intended to keep busy. The king's "apartment soirées," held each Monday, Wednesday, and Thursday from October to Easter, were meant to encourage the top-ranking nobility to loosen their purse strings.

# A MOST COMMODIOUS COMMODE

**DESK (1708), BY ANDRÉ CHARLES BOULLE**
ABUNDANCE ROOM
KING'S GRAND APARTMENT

In 1708, André Charles Boulle delivered two strange desks with drawers for Louis XIV's room at the Grand Trianon. These pieces of furniture didn't yet have a name; they were deemed extremely *commodes* (commodious), and this was the name by which they became known. These commodes, the first in history, perfectly illustrate the technique of polychrome veneer in tortoiseshell and copper marquetry which made the cabinetmaker famous. One characteristic of Boulle's work was the application of bronze on his pieces to protect the most delicate parts. Like the female sphinxes on the two famous commodes, furniture found itself taken over by mascarons, claws, friezes, and leaves in gilded bronze. Thanks to his creativity and the richness of his ornamentation, Boulle became the greatest cabinetmaker of his day, acquiring an international renown which contributed to the reputation of Versailles and the export of French luxury items throughout Europe. But rubbing shoulders with princes and the powerful incited him to become a collector himself, spending lavishly... until he was ruined. Only the king's intervention saved him from bankruptcy.

# THE CIRCLE
# OF VIRTUOUS COURTIERS

**CORNERS OF THE CEILING OF THE QUEEN'S GUARDS' ROOM**
QUEEN'S GRAND APARTMENT

Before being installed in the queen's apartments in 1680, this ceiling representing royal justice through the Jupiter myth was in the former Apartment of the Planets, in the Jupiter Room. When it was moved, it was probably slightly modified with the addition in the four corners of curious courtiers seemingly painted surreptitiously under drapery held by *putti*. Was there a reason these figures featured in this panegyric to royal temperance? Their presence necessarily signifies the court's orbit around the monarch. And yet, leaning lasciviously on the edge of a balustrade, these courtiers aren't looking at him but rather at the spectator. Did the painter intend to mock the court? Art was too controlled at

Versailles for it to be possible to take such a liberty. Therefore it should be seen rather as a sort of warning to courtiers, a reflection of their own image. While men at court often had to use artifice to please the king, he did not like being surrounded by superficial people. As taught in *The Book of the Courtier* by Italian diplomat Baldassare Castiglione (1528)—a de facto manual for learning proper behavior in European courts—, grace could only be virtuous if it was inhabited by a good mind and a certain morality. The court was both the king's instrument and his reflection, so the depiction of courtiers on this ceiling points courtly spectators towards going beyond mere appearances.

# THE LIVING AND THE DEAD

***THE ASSEMBLY OF THE GODS*** (1669)
ŒIL-DE-BŒUF ROOM
KING'S APARTMENT

This exceedingly strange painting was commissioned by Monsieur, brother of Louis XIV, for his Château de Saint-Cloud. A mixture of humanism and myths, it is an allegorical representation of the eighteen members of the royal family. The queen mother in the center, holding a globe as Cybele, goddess of the Earth, is framed by Monsieur as a morning star and Louis XIV as Jupiter. Behind her, the Three Graces are the Mesdemoiselles d'Orléans, daughters of Gaston, brother of Louis XIII, while the Grande Mademoiselle stands on the right, dressed as Diana. Sitting on the king's dais, the queen is depicted as Juno surrounded by her children, with the Dauphin holding her hand, the Petite Madame sitting at her feet, and the Duke of Anjou on her knees. On the left of the composition, holding Neptune's trident, we see Monsieur's mother-in-law, Henriette-Marie of France, as Amphitrite,

while on the right, Princess Henrietta of England, Monsieur's first wife, stands as Flora next to their eldest daughter, who appears dressed as Zephyrus. One year after this work was created, only the last of these women was still alive. But in truth, not all of the women represented were living when the painting was executed, because in the center we see the queen mother in front of one of the three dead Mesdemoiselles and, drawing a triangle, the grandchildren who died young. In the frame, we see the two daughters of Louis XIV, Anne-Élisabeth and Marie-Anne, and, on their right, the mourned son of Monsieur, Philippe-Charles, who is presenting his sister Anne-Marie with Apollo's lyre. Nor was the latter one of the dead when the work was painted, as it was in fact commissioned to celebrate her impending birth.

# THE KING'S
# REGARD

I n 1701, the first œil-de-bœuf window in this room, on the Queen's Courtyard side, was joined by a mirrored fellow on the side of the king's new room, in the name of symmetry. In combination with the "royal" fireplace with its great mirror to amplify the light, the oculus is particularly symbolic. It is part of the rituals of the king's rising and retiring; right where every day courtiers crowded in the passage between the two rooms, it marks a move from one world to another, between the profane and the sacred. Every morning around 8 o'clock, as soon as the Swiss Guard had put the bed away behind the screen (near the fireplace), the First Valet opened the door of the bedroom, crying "The wardrobe, gentlemen!" Then the blood princes and principal officers entered according to rank, bringing the king his shirt and helping him with his toilet. Next came the First Physician and the First Surgeon, the "commode carrier," as well as other high-ranking gentlemen. Then it was the turn of the Officers of the Chamber, pages, governors, squires... and so on and so forth, until the last of the privileged parties. Once the king was dressed, the two doors were opened to admit the rest of the courtiers. While they may have been unable to "get to the bottom of things," as Louis XIV said, they recounted "their views on what they saw outside, most often regarding precedence and rank."

At bedtime, around 11:30 p.m., the great parade started again, concluding with the candlestick ceremony: the king inspected the face of each person present, then indicated the person who, like the humblest of servants, would have the privilege of blowing out the flame when leaving the room. "The art of giving life to nothings," remarked Saint-Simon...

# THE SANCTUARY
# OF THE MONARCHY

**BED OF LOUIS XIV (RECONSTRUCTED IN 1980)**
KING'S BEDROOM
KING'S APARTMENT

S et in the center of the palace in 1701, Louis XIV's bedroom symbolizes the ritualization of court life around his person. The royal bed outclassed the throne, which was only used on rare occasions, notably when the king received extraordinary delegations in the Hall of Mirrors. Most audiences were held at the foot of the bed, which since medieval times had traditionally been seen as the seat of lordly power. Every morning after his prayers, Louis XIV held a first meeting with his ministers before the Council session. Besides members of the clergy, no one was allowed to approach the bed, which was separated from the rest of the room by a balustrade marking the line between the common area and the sacred area. Even when the king was absent, courtiers had to bow and ladies had to curtsy. Day and night, a valet guarded the royal bed and ushers made sure attitudes were worthy of the place.

The sumptuous decoration of this veritable "bed of State" attested to the sovereign presence invested by God during the coronation. As royalty never stops, it was in this room, towards which all eyes were turned, that it was proclaimed "The king is dead, long live the king!" on September 1, 1715, after Louis XIV's seventy-two-year reign.

# KING DAVID

The iconographic program of the Royal Chapel draws learned parallels between the Old and New Testaments which may seem enigmatic: for example, above the lamentation of Christ, Corneille Van Clève's high altar focuses glory on the Hebrew name of Yahweh. On the pillars framing the choir there are sculpted menorahs, the Tables of the Law and, the Ark of the Covenant, right next to the instruments of the Passion of Christ. On the organ case overlooking the musicians' and choristers' gallery of the Royal Chapel there is also a bas-relief featuring a crowned king playing a harp. This is King David, whose history is retraced in the Old Testament: king of the people of Israel, he imposed one God and made Jerusalem the capital of the kingdom by placing the sacred Ark of the Covenant there. Through Nathan's prophecy, God promised him a stable reign and line of descent. For Louis XIV, David was the great biblical figure with whom he wished to be associated. The link between the two sovereigns is also found in the role granted to the arts as instruments of power: David was a poet- and musician-king. The bas-relief on the organ in the Royal Chapel drawn by Robert de Cotte is oddly reminiscent of Dominiquin's *David Playing the Harp* (1620)—the king's favorite painting which can now be admired above the fireplace in the Mars Room. This may be Louis XIV's personal signature, placed on his last great architectural work, through which he celebrated the glory of the Almighty and the beauty of His creation.

# COURTLY SERVICES

**\*\* CALENDAR OF THE "ANNIVERSARIES OF THE KING'S CHAPEL"**
MUSICIANS' SACRISTY
ROYAL CHAPEL

In the sacristy serving the galleries of the Royal Chapel, a wardrobe built into the wall hides a touching souvenir of court life under Louis XV—a calendar of the commemorative Masses for the royal family which was rediscovered by chance a few years ago. It was updated for the death of Queen Marie Leszczynska, which dates it to about 1770. Home of the one said to be the "Most Christian King," Versailles was not just a place animated by the king's pleasures—celebrations, balls, and entertainment. Activities at the Royal Chapel were an integral part of daily life at the palace. There were religious ceremonies directly involving the royal family—baptisms, communions, weddings...—that no one could miss, but also important holy days in the Christian liturgy. The Royal Chapel was a model parish in the eyes of the kingdom and the heart of a prominent religious community run by the Lazarists. Already under Louis XIV it was in charge of holding ordinary and extraordinary services for the royal family's public worship as well as rituals celebrating the king's sacredness. His successors kept to that path. We don't know, however, why this calendar was not updated during the reign of Louis XVI.

# PEACE
# AND PROSPERITY!

**LOUIS XV OFFERING PEACE TO EUROPE (1729), BY FRANÇOIS LEMOINE**
PEACE ROOM

Above the fireplace in the Peace Room, which is at the end of the long symbolic enfilade starting at the War Room and opening onto the Queen's Grand Apartment, there is a vast oval painting featuring the eighteen-year-old Louis XV as an *imperator*. He is presenting an olive branch to Europe, while in the background Discord tries in vain to open the doors to the temple of Janus (closed in Rome in peace time). By his side, Fecundity and Piety hold two newborns, Louis XV's twin girls. How different from the work by Antoine Coysevox in the War Room representing *Louis XIV Victorious and Crowned by Glory* (1680)! Here, war propaganda gives way to a regard for peace as something sacred, marking a shift in values at the beginning of the 18<sup>th</sup> century. It's true that in 1686, Le Brun's ceiling paintings already showed a desire for peace, but the end of Louis XIV's reign was one long succession of wars that people perceived as genuine calamities. Thus was born the idea of a "perpetual peace" which would favor prosperity. Before his death, Louis XIV had warned his successor against wars waged for "vanity": "Don't imitate me, but be a peaceful prince, and may your main endeavor be to provide relief to your subjects." In the first years of his reign, Louis XV did indeed try to think of peace as the instrument of his glory.

# AS BLUE
# AS THE SKY

**APOTHEOSIS OF HERCULES (1733–1736)**
HERCULES ROOM

Anyone entering the Hercules Room will feel suddenly swept into this ascension scene. Painted over three years, François Lemoyne's *trompe-l'œil* ceiling is on a par with the neighboring ceilings by Le Brun and his allegories. Here, Hercules opens the doors to Olympus and immortality. The scene covers nearly 230 square meters and includes more than 140 figures! It was the first great monumental artistic undertaking of Louis XV's reign, even though the marble wall decoration completed in 1729 had been commissioned by Louis XIV. The placement of the huge Veronese painting, *The Meal at the House of Simon the Pharisee* (1576), in the Hercules Room had been planned ever since it was given to Louis XIV by the Republic of Venice in 1664.

But in 1739, during the inauguration of the room for the wedding of Louis XV's eldest daughter, all people talked about was Lemoyne's talent. That led the king to name him First Painter. Alas, a few months later, Lemoyne committed suicide by stabbing himself nine times with a sword. Many said that overwork, along with his wife's death, had driven him mad. While his perfectionism surely had something to do with his tragic death, there may have been other, more material reasons, as referred to by the Duke de Luynes: Lemoyne had only been paid 10,000 ecus for that painting, and his debts amounted to 29,000 *livres*, including 24,000 for the ultramarine blue alone which gave that ceiling its exceptional quality...

# A ROOM
# OF HIS OWN

When he arrived at Versailles in 1722 at the age of 12, Louis XV first lived in his great-grandfather's large central room. At 90 square meters, with 10-meter ceilings, the room was all the more difficult to heat in winter because it faced east. At the age of 27, the Well-Beloved King left it for a more comfortable south-facing room. Jacques Ange Gabriel and Jacques Verbeckt composed a remarkably simple decor for this new room: a white ceiling, bright and luminous, a cornice decorated with children playing and little birds flying, thin white panels finely sculpted with gilded Rococo floral motifs, and many mirrors that reflected the light. Needless to say, it was a break from Louis XIV-style monumentality.

And yet throughout his life, Louis XV bent to the requirements of Versailles ceremony, going to his forbear's room every morning for the rising ritual. Likewise, every night, after receiving the honors dictated by etiquette, he left the room in a housecoat. At the end of his reign, these comings and goings no longer fooled anyone, so the king died in his private bedroom on May 10, 1774. Nonetheless, the king did not occupy this room as a simple "bourgeois" for thirty-seven years. The place was invested with the solemnity associated with the royal function, and protocol was scrupulously observed there. The room which Louis XVI occupied after his grandfather remained one of those places in the palace where few mortals had the right to tread.

# THE KING'S TOWN HOUSE

**\* COURTYARD OF THE STAGS AND THE KING'S STAIRCASE**

When visitors are lucky enough to enter the Courtyard of the Stags, they discover the many floors and numerous windows of the private spaces which Louis XV built in the heart of the palace, away from prying eyes. The history of these places began after the Regency of the Duke of Orléans, with the arrival of the young king in Versailles in 1722.

Above the king's interior apartments, in which Louis XIV displayed his collections, the Regent created a first turning room under the eaves so Louis XV could learn to turn wood and ivory. This was the first of the private facilities which the sovereign constantly extended and developed as he imagined them. As space was limited, he decided to encroach on the two inner courtyards which his great-grandfather had left him and built three floors invisible from the Marble Courtyard or the Royal Courtyard. This operation created many small rooms, libraries, and dining rooms in which Louis XV could receive those close to him. The summer dining room on the fourth floor opened onto vast terraces, aviaries, laboratories and other "cabinets of curiosities." The whole worked autonomously, with its own kitchens, servants, and entrances. Built in 1754, the King's Staircase—the main staircase by which one reached the Guards' Apartment from the Royal Courtyard—was a way to avoid the official apartments and the courtier-cluttered Queen's Staircase.

# ROYAL DOGHOUSE

**\* CORNICE OF FIRST ANTECHAMBER OF THE KING'S APARTMENTS**

When Louis XV took possession of Louis XIV's former billiard room to make it his bedroom in 1737, he had most of the 1684 decoration transferred to this room, asking Jacques Ange Gabriel and Jacques Verbeckt to update it. As the room was meant to be used as an entrance to the interior apartments, Louis XV decided it would be a good idea to preserve some of the paneling, particularly the cornice depicting an innocent hunting scene in which children accompanied by bloodhounds track a deer. Louis XV had his favorite dogs sleep in a few doghouses set along the walls of this antechamber!

Given the small size of the room, it wasn't a whole pack, but rather a few animals chosen by the king when he returned from a hunt. The others were returned to the royal kennel in town (on the site of current Prefecture). What wouldn't courtiers have given for such an honor! In the evening, the king took care of his dogs according to a well-established ritual: if he wanted to give them a few *gimblettes*—little dry ring-shaped biscuits—, he could not do so with his own hands, but had to delegate the task to the Grand Master or, in his absence, to the First Maître d'Hôtel.

# DINNERS FOR
# THE FAVORED FEW

**\*DINING ROOM FOR RETURNING HUNTING PARTIES**
KING'S INTERIOR APARTMENTS

Until 1769, this space, one of Louis XV's private dining rooms, decorated in 1750, was where dinners were held when he returned from hunting expeditions. Besides an account by the Duke of Croÿ, we know barely any details about these much-desired evenings which began in the 1730s. These private suppers were held as the king saw fit, gathering twenty guests, very few of them women, for their voluminous dresses prevented them from moving around in these small rooms. Louis XV wanted to distinguish a few gentlemen and appreciate the value of their company. Freeing himself of the court's official workings and his rightful privileges, Louis XV was once again in control, shaking up habits. The invention of this increasingly discreet court life was not only the sign of a new sociability, but also an indication of the strengthening of absolute power. These suppers were nevertheless only private in appearance; in reality they were as formidable as those instituted by Louis XIV in The Grand Trianon or Marly.

# A WHIFF
# OF SCANDAL

**\* ROOM IN MADAME DE POMPADOUR'S APARTMENT**
KING'S SMALL APARTMENT (ATTIC)

After Marie Leszczynska closed her door to him following her successive pregnancies, Louis XV had his first extramarital liaisons with four sisters from a very aristocratic family: Louise, Pauline, Diane, and Marie-Anne de Mailly-Nesle. Hiding these dalliances, he housed them discreetly, by turns, in tiny rooms (now destroyed) adjoining his Small Apartment above the War Room. Nonetheless, Marie-Anne managed to make her position official; in 1743, she was given the title Duchess of Châteauroux and Louis XV granted her a small but comfortable six-room apartment in the attic suite. She barely had time to enjoy it, however, because she died of peritonitis the next year. A scandal occurred in August 1743 when the king, on a military campaign in Metz, fell gravely ill. As he hovered between life and

death, his First Chaplain refused to give him absolution without a public confession of his sins and the dismissal of his mistress. The sermon soon made its way all over France. Healthy again and back at Versailles, the humiliated Louis XV banished the chaplain to his diocese and recalled his darling Madame de Châteauroux, not realizing he would never see her again. This cabal, in which the aristocracy had participated, left a profound impression on the king, and all the mistresses he chose thereafter were commoners. The first among them, Madame de Pompadour, née Jeanne Antoinette Poisson, arrived at court in 1745 as a complete unknown. Louis XV set her up in the former apartment of the Duchess of Châteauroux, and she spent her first five years at Versailles there.

# WELL-HOUSED
## *OR NOT*

**\*\* MADAME DU HAUSSET'S ROOM**
MADAME DE POMPADOUR'S APARTMENT
KING'S SMALL APARTMENT (ATTIC)

Adjacent to Madame de Pompadour's apartment there is a small room fitted with closets used as wardrobes. From there, a small staircase rises to the entresol, up to a dark room, soberly furnished, with a very low ceiling—1.75 meters—,fairly characteristic of the living conditions of the *bien-logés* (well-housed). It was the room of the Marquise's servant, a certain Madame du Hausset, famous for her *Memoirs* which drew a merciless portrait of the court of Louis XV: intrigue, lies, trickery, and morals corrupted by money, power, sex, and ambition. Although the text was certainly rewritten after her death by Gabriel Sénac de Meilhan to create

a publishing sensation in 1824, it was nonetheless at least partly true, providing a different view of Versailles and revealing the bitterness of this woman housed in cramped rooms. And yet, she fared better than others. Many had to be content with the Grand Commun, the Stables, or the royal kennel. When there was no more space, a meager allowance was provided for the rental of a tiny room in a private home or a room at an inn. All these "poorly-housed" persons were dubbed *galopins*: a pejorative term which, under Louis XIV, was used for kitchen boys, referring to anyone, humble servant or visiting noble, who did not have the privilege of being housed by the king.

# A POSE
# OF PIETY

## * MADAME DE POMPADOUR'S PRIVATE ORATORY
ROYAL CHAPEL

From 1750 onwards, Madame de Pompadour was no more than a friend and confidante to Louis XV. Therefore, she left her attic apartment to move to the ground floor of the palace, near the king's daughters. While some thought this meant she was in disgrace, she later confirmed her new favor. In 1752, she was given the title of duchess. There were more and more insulting pamphlets which denounced her power and her hold over the king: the famous poissonades (a term derived from the Duchess's maiden name "Poisson" and alluding to the mazarinades that satirized Cardinal Mazarin in the 18th century). Madame de Pompadour undertook to modify her image and, following the illustrious example of Madame de Maintenon, she decided to become devout. The private oratory she had built in the Royal Chapel became the instrument of this change. Not only did the oratory allow her to discreetly attend religious services, but also to be seen through its white window! In 1756, the king granted her a post as the queen's "Lady of the Palace" and she took a Jesuit as her confessor. Alas, her devoutness fooled no one. La Pompadour remained a bonne vivante, more enamored of theater, philosophy, and art than of spiritual retreat and prayers. If she managed to remain the main mistress for so long, it was because she, of all the king's entourage, had a bright, playful mind of which Louis XV never tired. In April 1764, as she lay dying, the king allowed her to remain at Versailles, although it was forbidden for anyone not of royal blood to die there. Seeing the cart carrying her body leaving the palace, Louis XV declared: "This is the only honor I was able to give my friend of twenty years."

# MARIE, QUEEN OF FRANCE

*THE FARM* (1750), BY MARIE LESZYNSKA

BEDROOM OF THE DAUPHIN'S APARTMENT

This little painting signed "Marie, Queen of France" is practically all that remains at Versailles of the works of Louis XV's wife. It is a copy of a painting the dauphin had ordered from Jean-Baptiste Oudry, who gave his mother painting lessons. This agricultural and rustic composition reflects the simple virtues cultivated by Marie Leszczynska, described as a "mystical queen"—shutting herself in her rooms for hours each day to pray—and a devoted mother. Nevertheless, just like Louis XV, Marie Leszczynska maintained a social circle including great minds, particularly to indulge in her greatest passion: listening to music. She invited renowned artists to the palace, like Farinelli

the castrato, who gave her singing lessons in 1752. The queen loved holding these "little concerts" or putting on plays and was assuredly one of the main patrons of cultural life at Versailles. History has focused more on the role played by Madame de Pompadour, undoubtedly because of Marie Leszczynska's relegation to the fringe of court life, where she had no privileged access to power and favors. Unlike the king, she had no small private apartment spacious enough to accommodate her faithful inner circle, so the queen was often forced to hold her soirées at the home of the Duchess of Luynes, her lady-in-waiting, who had a charming apartment in the South Wing.

# A KING'S SON, A KING'S FATHER, NEVER A KING

**LIBRARY**
DAUPHIN'S APARTMENT

This library furnished around 1750 was the place where Louis XV's son, the dauphin Louis-Ferdinand, worked before his death. After he died, it served the same purpose for the future Louis XVI, the dauphin Louis Auguste. Well before their time, the first occupant had been the Grand Dauphin, the eldest son of Louis XIV, of whom there remains no trace here, except perhaps the famous little *caveau*, a dark back room in which he spent his days reading *Mercure de France*, books on hunting, summaries of operas... Of all these heirs apparent to the throne, many waited in vain for the reign promised them by their birth. The Grand Dauphin died at the age of 49 in 1711, four years before Louis XIV, while his son Philip V had taken the Spanish throne. There was a court saying: "A king's son, a king's father, never a king." Louis-Ferdinand, the eldest son of Louis XV, also experienced this abortive destiny full of frustration and bitterness. Reduced to the role of a bit player by his own father, with whom he did not get along and of whose private life he disapproved, he only belatedly joined the Council in 1757, at the age of 28, after proving his bravery by overpowering the regicidal Damiens. He died of tuberculosis in 1765, at the age of 36.

\* *Caveau* of the Grand Dauphin.

# THE KING'S
# SECRET

## * ROLL-TOP WRITING DESK OR KING'S DESK (1760–1769)
### CORNER ROOM
### KING'S INTERIOR APARTMENTS

The "king's desk" is one of the most famous pieces of furniture in the world. Commissioned in 1760 by Louis XV from the cabinetmaker Jean-François Œben, it was only completed in 1769 by Jean-Henri Riesener, after mobilising the work of fourteen trades! The refinement of its wood marquetry (sycamore, kingwood, and mahogany) and its chased bronzes are as impressive as the precision of its workings: just a quarter turn of a key is enough to simultaneously release or block the roll top and the drawers. Imported into France by Austrian ambassador Wenzel Anton von Kaunitz mid-century, this roll-top desk system is the most advanced ever designed

Without its key, this writing desk became a real vault.
Even the staff who restocked it with paper and ink could only do so through a small concealed hatch. State secrets being a part of life, it served the confidentiality of a monarch shut away in his work room to govern independently of the Council. Louis XV only rarely received his ministers for private audiences in this room, and even less often in the adjoining room behind it, the Cabinet des Dépêches (Dispatch Room), where he pored over reports from his spies. This mysterious double diplomacy allowed him to short-circuit official policy and earned the name of "the king's secret."

# STARS IN
# HIS EYES

## * PASSEMANT'S ASTRONOMICAL CLOCK (1730–1740))
CLOCK ROOM
KING'S INTERIOR APARTMENTS

It took engineer Claude Siméon Passemant and clockmaker Louis Dauthiau nearly nineteen years to create this extraordinary astronomical clock presented to the Royal Academy of Sciences in 1749. Given to Louis XV in 1754, it was placed in this room which then took its name, after bronze-smiths Jacques and Philippe Caffieri enhanced its appearance. Every December 31, Louis XV enjoyed being with his family to observe the change to the New Year as it appeared on the clock face (it takes into account leap years and is programmed to work until the year 9999!). On a more daily basis, he liked to watch through the crystal globe as the planets revolved around the sun, as Copernicus had established. It was a far cry from the simple automaton clock which Antoine Morand had given to Louis XIV in 1706 (Mercury Room). Passemant and Dauthiau's extraordinarily accurate astronomical clock was the product of the technical and scientific advances of the Enlightenment. It was used to set the first official time for the kingdom. In the same room, you can also see a copper line embedded in the parquet floor; this was used to tell time by the Versailles meridian every day when a ray hit the hole in the metal plate nailed to the window. Louis XV became interested in astronomy at the age of 14; the young man had the astronomers Jacques Cassini and Jacques Philippe Maraldi come to Versailles to observe a total eclipse of the sun on May 22, 1724 and take measurements. Thanks to the telescopes Passemant made for him, the king was able to devote himself to his passion his whole life long, keeping up with Royal Academy of Sciences publications like a true scholar.

# A FAMILY
## OF MUSIC LOVERS

Although Louis XIV could play the mandolin, under his reign music was still mainly left to the experts. Under Louis XV, however, it became a means of socializing for the royal family. Supervised first by music master Baptiste Matho, then Pancrace Royer, the royal children reached almost professional proficiency. Be it the Dauphin, who sang beautifully, or Mesdames, the whole family shared this enthusiasm. Paintings by Jean-Marc Nattier depict Louis XV's daughters with their favorite instruments. The woodwork in the apartments also alludes to this musical inclination, like the woodwork in the Madame Victoire's Grand Cabinet created in 1763. In that room, you can even see the harpsichord built for her by François-Étienne Blanchet. Furthermore, Madame Victoire was the most gifted of all, widely celebrated by the composers of the time. In 1764, Mozart dedicated his *First Sonata* Work to her, and in 1751, Couperin dedicated his *Book of Harpsichord Pieces* to her. Madame Henriette excelled at playing the viola, and Madame Adélaïde, whose professor was Beaumarchais, was a talented harpist, and also played the violin and the organ (the latter remains in her "grand cabinet"). It is said Louis XV was in the habit of coming to see them for the simple pleasure of having coffee and listening to them. This practice of playing music in private did not bring renown to Versailles; in the 18th century, modernity was to be found in Paris.

It is for this reason, for example, that after his sixteen-day stay at Versailles in late 1763, Mozart turned down the king's offer of a job as organist of the Royal Chapel.

# THE GODS WATCH
# OVER THE OPERA HOUSE

**\*\* NORTH FAÇADE OF THE ROYAL OPERA**

Standing at the foot of the reservoirs which supply the garden's fountains, this façade with its ravishing sculpted decoration constitutes the missing piece of Louis XIV's palace, the part which remained unfinished for lack of funds. Nearly eighty years later, Louis XV chose to build the Royal Opera (1768–1770) on the same spot. The steep drop from the terrain on which the North Wing and reservoirs were built allowed for a substantial space under the stage. As the opera house was entirely built of wood and lit with 3,000 candles, there had to be water nearby in case of fire. Therefore, particular attention was paid to the building's design. Jacques Ange Gabriel opted for a stone shell around the opera which, although it might not save the hall, would prevent the

flames from reaching the rest of the palace. The masonry work was done between 1764 and 1765, even before there was an overall plan for the space. In 1769, the sculpture on the north façade was entrusted to Augustin Pajou and Jules-Antoine Rousseau. The pediment of the avant-corps features *Lyric Poetry* as a young woman crowned with laurels and playing the lyre, sitting amidst thick clouds from which cherubs arise. Apollo, Mars, and Minerva preside over the keystones of the ground-floor arcades and the upper windows. The reservoir terraces, with the actors' building along the left side, were no more accessible to the public then than they are today, so ultimately, this ravishing sculpted decoration is only for the benefit of the north wind.

# ALL THE WORLD'S A STAGE

Louis XIV almost always observed court ceremony, but Louis XV cultivated a certain distance from obligations to appear. For his opera house, for example, he asked Jacques Ange Gabriel to set him aside three discreet, comfortable boxes closed off with grilles from which he could watch performances almost incognito, accompanied by those close to him and his ministers. The grand royal box that was planned was therefore never created, even though, for visual effect, its placement was marked by Charles de Wailly by an ellipse in the colonnade. In the opera house's iconography, Louis XV's figure is likewise absent. With little interest in glorifying his person, the king had more affinity with the decorative arts to which he attributed the role of flattering the mind and the senses.

Created in 1769 by the painter Claude-Joseph Vernet, the decor of the three boxes, which seem more like boudoirs, was therefore a celebration of sensual beauty in allegorical form. Intertwined with exquisite grotesques, the king's box has birds pecking at the embrasure of its grille, while winged mermaids present vases and baskets of fruit in a sea of flowered branches and ribbons. The two other boxes for ministers are rife with motifs of flowers and vine branches, bacchantes, shepherdesses, huntresses, Nereids, Amazons, and other half-naked nymphs, evoking actresses as one might dream of them. These shocked Louis-Philippe so greatly he had them whitewashed over. Luckily, the first restoration of the hall between 1952 and 1956 uncovered them once again.

# BEHIND
## THE ILLUSION

**\*\* AREA UNDER THE STAGE (RESTORED IN 2003–2009)**
ROYAL OPERA

naugurated in 1770 on the occasion of the wedding of the Dauphin and Marie-Antoinette, the Royal Opera rapidly became one of the most famous performance halls in Europe. Its remarkable sculpted wood decoration, wonderfully imitating marble and stone, make it a masterwork by the ornamentalists of Versailles. In addition, like the resonance chamber of an instrument, it offers perfect acoustics. What makes this opera house truly exceptional, however, is the system of invisible mechanics of the area under the stage which permitted the most fabulous artifice. Ten-meter panels could appear and disappear before spectators' eyes, activated by a finely tuned system of counterweights on pulleys manipulated from a wheel shaft such as was found on ships. The inventiveness of the mechanisms made it possible to change the scenery in no time at all. Likewise, in the hall, a moveable floor could be lowered and raised using a jack; this way, the opera house could be used for balls and feasts. Those responsible were the engineers and architects of the Menus-Plaisirs, particularly the First Machinist to the King, Blaise-Henri Arnoult, who had already distinguished himself by creating the collapsible theater of the Ambassadors' Staircase for Madame de Pompadour. Nevertheless, the mechanisms we now see in the famous space under the Royal Opera could only be partially saved. However, Arnoult had a student as brilliant as he, Pierre Boullet, who in 1779 created the machinery for the Petit Trianon theater for Marie-Antoinette. Luckily, that machinery is still in perfect working order.

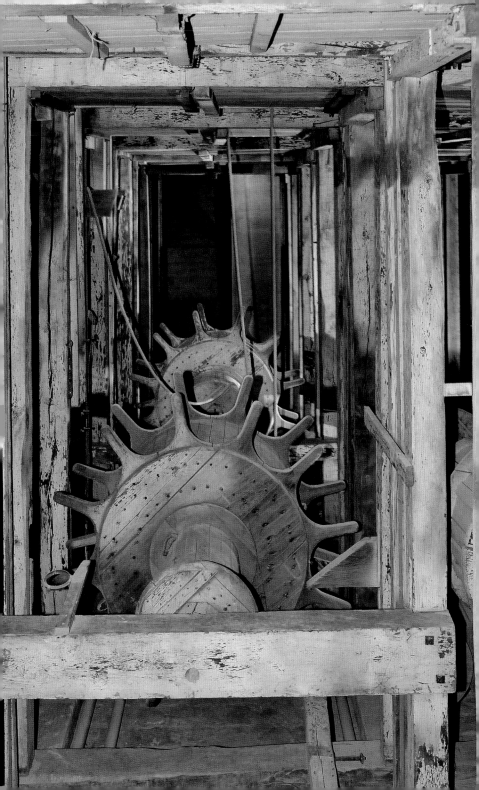

# AT HOME
## WITH HIS MISTRESS

**\* MADAME DU BARRY'S LIBRARY AND BATHROOM**
KING'S SMALL APARTMENT (3RD FLOOR)

Before becoming Louis XV's mistress in April 1769, Jeanne Bécu was a salesgirl in a fashion boutique on Rue Saint-Honoré in Paris. Married for form's sake to a certain Count du Barry before being introduced to court, she was met with only disdain and hostility. Conscious of the scandal the presence of this 25-year-old commoner could cause, Louis XV sought to protect her by setting her up discreetly in his Small Apartment. They lived there in relative privacy, keeping company with a few people, far from the scrutiny of the court. To create his mistress' apartment, the king cleared seven rooms which were then partially renovated: two small rooms, a dining room, a bedroom, a bathroom, a games room, and a library. Set on the third floor under the eaves of the old palace, they have low ceilings which make them feel more private and lend them the appearance of simplicity. The furniture and decors were nonetheless just as refined and luxurious and those of the apartments on the second floor, the watchwords here being comfort and autonomy. In winter, heating was partially provided by stoves, which retained heat longer; the king prepared his own coffee there in a small cubbyhole within the tiny games room, set under the eaves. Madame du Barry's apartment was used most in winter, because in the spring, the king and his entourage moved to the "countryside," to the Petit Trianon. It was at the latter, on April 26, 1774, that Louis XV displayed the first symptoms of the smallpox which was to end his life two weeks later, with his mistress at his side.

# A PALACE WITHOUT CONVENIENCES?

L egend often had it that Versailles was terribly dirty and malodorous. Doubtless, as the palace—open every day to thousands of visitors and inhabited by hundreds of people—sometimes left something to be desired as far as cleanliness was concerned. Nevertheless, hygiene was a consideration of the first order. From the reign of Louis XIV, the palace had public latrines in the attics, and each person with official lodgings had his or her own *chaise d'affaires* (literally, "chair for business"). However, it wasn't until the end of the reign of Louis XV that there were private conveniences, like the one adjoining Dispatch Room which retains, in addition to a commode attributed to Gaudreaux, a luxurious bidet in rosewood veneer and kingwood marquetry by Bernard II Van Risen Burgh. Later, under Louis XVI, the first hydraulic commodes with siphons, invented by Alexander Cummings in 1775, were installed, linked to a reservoir in the entresol and leakproof tanks. This development put an end to the medical prescription of attentive study of feces, particularly royal ones, to gauge the humors of the mind and body. The new hydraulic commodes described by the Count of Hezecques in his memoirs must certainly have resembled the one fitted with a mahogany flap located in the second room adjoining the Dispatch Room. Louis-Philippe had it installed in the early 1830s to replace the old mechanism which disappeared during the revolutionary sell-off. The same goes for the one in the queen's inner chambers, installed for Queen Marie-Amélie.

# ROYAL VAPORS

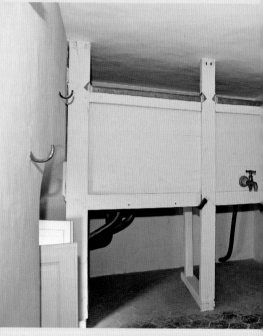

Although the practice of taking baths only became common in the 19th century, it was fairly popular within the royal family's entourage, becoming an envied and sought-after court privilege. The traditional "dry toilet"—which consisted of rubbing oneself with a perfumed cloth—was gradually abandoned in favor of baths, which no longer had to be medically prescribed. Of course, under Louis XV, baths were taken clothed and seated under a cloth tent, but the relationship to water changed completely; little by little, people came around to the idea that water was part of good hygiene and wasn't harmful to health,

whereas previously people had believed that miasmas were transmitted through dilated pores and that immersion filled the body with vapor. Louis XV was the first to have rooms created which were very comfortable and modern for the time: no water-bearers, but instead real taps which carried water through copper piping tucked behind the wooden paneling from the tanks in the entresol, heated by a brazier and fitted with a vent to evacuate the steam. Louis XV's sixth bathroom, created in 1765, is unusual in that it was fitted with two bathtubs, although we don't really know in whose company the king used them. The

practice of taking baths became a new *art de vivre* which, with Marie-Antoinette, rose to great heights of refinement. The large bathroom she ordered from Richard Mique in 1784 was embellished with a decor of swans drinking from ponds, reeds, dolphins, shells, pearls, and branches of coral, which entertained her during extended moments of relaxation. Proof that this was not just a form of relaxation for women alone: the magnificent daybed in the room came from Louis XVI's bathroom in Fontainebleau!

* Bathroom in the Queen's Small Apartment
Ornamentalists: Jules Hugues and Jean Siméon Rousseau, under the direction of Richard Mique.

# JOURNEY
## AROUND THE WORLD

**\* DECORATIVE MEDALLIONS BY JULES ANTOINE ROUSSEAU AND HIS SONS**
LOUIS XV'S SEVENTH BATHROOM (WHICH BECAME LOUIS XVI'S CABINET DE LA CASSETTE)
KING'S INTERIOR APARTMENTS

The Cabinet de la Cassette, so named because Louis XVI kept his records and his private accounts (*la cassette*) there, was the most beautiful of Louis XV's bathrooms. Its wooden panels feature a multitude of gilded medallions, bordered with reeds and narcissi, which evoke the pleasures of the water: bathing, fishing, hunting aquatic birds, and swimming. These scenes in praise of life outdoors reflect debates on the ideas of "freedom" and nature in fashion in the philosophical salons of the day. They also reveal the era's enthusiasm for travel accounts littered with descriptions of "noble savages" living far from social conventions.

In the early 1770s, the explorers Louis Antoine de Bougainville and Jean-François de La Pérouse returned from their maritime journeys with drawings, scientific facts, and accounts which whetted people's curiosity: *Le Voyage autour du monde* by Bougainville, who discovered Tahiti in 1768, was a great publishing success, notably thanks to its descriptions of loose morals between the two sexes and their osmosis with nature. Depicting naked men and women swimming together innocently, the medallions in the bathroom created in 1771 are steeped in the Tahitian ideal, recreated here with an almost ethnographic focus on precision. This masterpiece is all the more important because it marks the emergence of a new style at Versailles which was to grow under Louis XVI—and bear his name—, a style in which the clean lines of the classical ideal were allied with simple, realistic naturalism.

# A PASSION FOR GEOGRAPHY

### ** MOVABLE GLOBE (1784)
#### VESTIBULE OF THE PROVENCE STAIRCASE
#### SOUTH WING

If he hadn't become king, Louis XVI might have become a cartographer, sailor, or explorer. Without a doubt, he knew more than anyone on those subjects, after the scientists of his time. Enthusiastic since his adolescence and trained by marine draftsman Nicolas Ozanne, he liked to dream about maritime spaces unknown to man which could not yet be represented on maps. From his rooms decked with measuring equipment and instruments, some newly invented, he contributed to scientific advances. For example, he participated in preparations for Jean-François de La Pérouse's voyage around the world to map the Pacific.

For the library in his interior apartments, he asked Jean-Henri Riesener to make a large table on which geographical maps could be corrected; consisting of a tabletop 2.10 meters in diameter cut from a single piece of Brazilian cedar, it was mounted on cylinders to stabilize the measuring instruments. For the dauphin's education, he even had many extremely precise globes made, like the extraordinary transformable globe by Mancelle, visible in the large room on the ground floor, which provided a speculative view of the ocean floor, with its relief drawn on a second inner sphere. Even more astonishing is the large movable globe with a circumference of 8.17 meters ordered in 1784 from the learned Le Clerc *père et fils*, Robert de Vaugondy, and Buache. However, this geographer king, fascinated with distant horizons and staunchly supportive of the Royal Navy, only saw the sea for the first time in June 1786, when he traveled to Normandy with the royal family to inaugurate the military port of Cherbourg.

# THE RETURN OF
# AN EXILE

**\*\* GRAND CABINET**
APARTMENT OF THE COUNT OF MAUREPAS
KING'S SMALL APARTMENT (3RD FLOOR)

As soon as he ascended to the throne, Louis XVI drove off Madame du Barry and took possession of his grandfather's Small Apartment for his First Valet Marc-Antoine Thierry, Baron of Ville d'Avray, and Count of Maurepas, whom he recalled from his forced exile on a suggestion from his aunts. This former Secretary of State for the Navy, disgraced in 1749 for his satirical poems about Madame de Pompadour, became the young king's mentor. Until his death in 1781, Maurepas shared his private life as de facto First Minister and was very involved in the major decisions early in the reign which were to have major consequences. While Maurepas' return to Versailles signified a return to morality—the end of the coteries run by mistresses—, he paradoxically contributed to consolidat-ing the court system for the new intrigues which were woven in this almost secret apartment sometimes served only personal interests. The great cycle of favors which made and unmade careers was still firmly in place. Furthermore, Maurepas was not a great advisor, bringing out Louis XVI's reluctance and procrastination at a time when the kingdom's financial situation was extremely critical. In this century of Enlightenment in which absolutism was more and more contested and in which people clamored for inspired governance, the opacity which surrounded the king's choices only made the situation worse. Versailles, once the most beautiful creation of the absolute monarchy, was becoming its tomb.

# A SMALL ENCYCLOPEDIC VOLUME

W as Louis XVI an enlightened king? The last masterwork by the Rousseau brothers created in 1788 seems to attest to this. The sculpted decor of this *studiolo*, where the king liked to work alone at dawn after rising discreetly, features musical instruments and the tools of painters, gardeners, and architects, but also equipment for lifting and experimentation, instruments for measurement and observation... and even an electrical machine. In this way, this little room pays homage to the quintessential eighteenth-century book, *the Encyclopedia*. Although the reign of Louis XVI may not have seen the desired reforms come to fruition, it was placed under the sign of knowledge. Can we ever say enough about the king's taste for apprenticeship and learning? All his life, Louis XVI taught himself whatever he deemed useful, be it sciences or languages—English, Italian, and Spanish. The catalogue of his library, established during the Revolution, counted 15,000 works in total. Court celebrations became learned, as on September 19, 1783, when the king had Joseph Montgolfier's aerostat tested: the balloon rose to 480 meters above the roofs of Versailles for ten minutes, carrying a rooster, a duck, and a sheep. Less than a year later, on June 23, 1784, it was the turn of the chemist and intendant of the royal family's scientific cabinets, François Pilâtre de Rozier, and the chemist Louis Proust to rise to 3,000 meters on board a hot-air balloon dubbed *Marie-Antoinette*, under the wondering gaze of the courtiers and the King of Sweden.

# THE KEYS
# TO COMMON LIFE

**\*\* LOUIS XVI'S WORKSHOP**
KING'S SMALL APARTMENT (3RD FLOOR)

Like his grandfather before him, Louis XVI set up a workshop in the Small Apartment for his physics and chemistry experiments and his woodworking. He also used the workshop for clockmaking, and locksmithing which he developed with François Gamain, perfecting equipment and techniques—thanks to foundry work carried out in the little forge under the roofs—to create mechanisms and prototype combination or "secret" locks. This enduring passion began when he was very young, thanks to lessons from Pierre Le Roy, expert in marine clockwork, as well as from brothers Nicolas and Louis Gamain (the father of François), the ironworkers and locksmiths of Louis XV. There was much talk about this king whose taste for common activities was seen as unforgiveable. The image presented by Louis XVI was not that expected of someone at court. His atypical personality did however express a certain idea of power which involved distancing himself from the superficiality and tyranny of fashion which reigned at court. By wrong-footing current values and vanities, by breaking with social habits and cultivating the image of a learned, solitary king, Louis XVI carried out a little palace revolution just as important as that of the frivolous Marie-Antoinette. However, by breaking the codes and traditions in favor of a little freedom, the royal couple lost all credibility in the exercise of power.

\*\* Forge of Louis XVI, King's Small Apartment, 5th floor.

# PRECIOUS PORCELAIN

**\* PORCELAIN DINING ROOM**
KING'S INTERIOR APARTMENTS

The last dining room used by Louis XV for his post-hunt suppers became, under Louis XVI, an official dining room. This retreat from court life into a room less than 81 meters square in the king's interior apartments marked the completion of his gradual privatization. Nevertheless, this dining room was certainly more appropriate than the Grand Apartment for some purposes. For example, every Christmas the king and queen held a major exhibition-sale there of the most remarkable porcelain pieces from the royal factory in Sèvres. The excellence of the factory, recognized in all the courts of Europe, including Russia—in 1778, Catherine the Great ordered no fewer than 744 pieces—, relied on major research into achieving hard porcelain, of which only

the "Orientals" had held the secret up until then. It was the 1768 discovery of the first kaolin deposit, near Limoges, which made Sèvres' fortune. Soft-paste porcelain— a mixture of white Marne limestone, sand, and sea salt homogenized by the addition of soap and glue, then shaped before firing—did however persist for decorative un-enameled "biscuit" objects. Prized for their finesse, they gradually replaced marble for portrait sculpture. Likewise, they took the place of the allegorical figures made from sugar placed on tables during society dinners in order to spark conversation among the guests.

# THE CABINET
## OF DREAMS

**\*REAR-CABINET OR POETS' CABINET**
QUEEN'S INNER ROOMS

This tiny room is an eloquent example of the little private space queens and dauphines had at their disposal. They had to make do with dark little rooms behind their official apartments. To cheer up these interiors which opened onto a narrow courtyard, they usually chose light-colored or gilded wood against a white background. However, in 1728 the Martin brothers invented a varnish which imitated Chinese lacquer and which was applied on furniture; it became very popular and was soon used on woodwork. After being glued on surfaces which had been fired, sheets of paper were decorated with painted scenes, then varnished with several coats of copal (a resin) before being glazed with gum arabic, which made them shine. Enlivened with floral compositions, these decors leaned heavily towards then-fashionable pastoral and bucolic scenes, in the manner of the painters Oudry, Boucher, and Fragonard, or Toile de Jouy fabric. The dauphine and mother of Louis XVI, Maria Josepha von Sachsen, particularly enjoyed these, as evidenced by the decor of panel which Marie-Antoinette had brought up beside her Golden Cabinet to replace the former Poets' Cabinet of Marie Leszczynska, for whom much of the woodwork decor had been delivered in 1729, upon the birth of the dauphin. The room was barely 2 or 3 meters square, so we can assume it was reserved for intimate conversations, reading, or daydreaming.

# SLEEPING
# IN STYLE

**MARIE-ANTOINETTE'S BED (RESTORED IN 1974)**
QUEEN'S CHAMBER
QUEEN'S GRAND APARTMENT

The queen's bedroom has been restored to the state in which Marie-Antoinette left it on October 6, 1789. We can see the "summer furniture" delivered in 1787, featuring magnificent half-damask fabric whose white background is embroidered with lilacs, ribbons, and peacock feathers, as well as much of the furniture she abandoned. This canopy bed is based on the model created by Jacques Gondoin in 1769, a few months before Marie-Antoinette arrived in France. A rooster and two turtle doves framed by two imperial eagles refer to the fact that the children to be born of this union between two foreign dynasties would be French. As pampered as they could be, the queens and dauphines only owed their position in court to their marriage and children. This maternal imperative led, for example, to the breaking of the engagement between Louis XV (11 years old) and Marie-Anne Victoire de Bourbon (3 years old) when it was realized that prospective descendents were distant indeed with such a young betrothed. The infant was sent back to Spain to be replaced by a 22-year-old princess, Marie Leszczynska, for whom much of the woodwork was delivered in 1729 when the dauphin was born. Remembrance of these two queens, however important it may be, must not distract us from the fact that in this dynastic room, nineteen royal children were born, including Philip V of Spain and Louis XV.

# WILD ABOUT
## TAPESTRY

**\* WHITE SATIN HALF-DAMASK WITH MEDALLIONS**
BILLIARD ROOM
QUEEN'S INNER ROOMS (3<sup>RD</sup> FLOOR)

I n the early 1780s, Marie-Antoinette, wishing to change her interiors, had the decors from previous reigns updated. She ordered new classical woodwork, giving carte blanche to Richard Mique and the Frères Rousseau, as well as tapestries of floral silk on light backgrounds, the fashion of the day. Satisfied with the result in her small inner rooms and in the Petit Trianon, in 1785 she decided to tackle the Grand Apartment. She asked Richard Mique to remove the wall marbles in the Nobles room and replace them with large sober woodwork frames hung with an apple-green damask

bordered with a wide golden braid. Other projects, like the decoration of the ante-chamber of the Grand Couvert and the Peace Room, were interrupted by the Revolution. This decorative fervor manifested itself fairly late in the reign; for almost ten years, Marie-Antoinette made no changes to the decor left her by Marie Leszczynska. It took eight long years for the queen to give birth to her first girl, a wait which made her a resident on borrowed time. The birth of the dauphin Louis-Joseph in 1781 finally gave her the legitimacy to impose her tastes.

111

# FOR THE LOVE
# OF TRANQUILITY

**\*MERIDIAN ROOM**
QUEEN'S INNER ROOMS

The Meridian Room ordered from Richard Mique in 1781 expresses Marie-Antoinette's need for privacy. It is special in that once the glass doors of the mirrored niche are closed, cut-out sections of the niche allowed the queen's servants to reach the other cubicles of her inner rooms from the bedroom without ever passing through this particular room. "Meridian" refers to rest taken during the median hours of the day. North-facing and open onto the interior courtyard, it was an ideal place to relax in the hottest hours of the summer. In the late spring of 1781, when the queen was entering the last months of her second pregnancy, the renovation was completed. The queen could shut herself in with the interior bolts marked with her monogram which complemented the locks.

Among the gilded bronzes applied to the glass doors by the carver-foundryman Pierre-Auguste Forestier, we find flowering rosebushes around the edges, an eagle with a club caught in branches, while the crowning element is a dolphin (*dauphin* in French) symbolizing the much-awaited birth. The pierced hearts level with the bolts are run through with a royal scepter with fleur de lys, expressing the king's love and protection as a warning to those who might think to disturb the queen's rest.

# GOLDEN
## NOTES

**\*GOLDEN CABINET**
QUEEN'S INNER ROOMS

The decor ordered from Richard Mique in 1783 was supposed to bring brightness and light into this dark room. The big mirrors reflect each other and the design of the woodwork sculpted with palmettes, sphinxes, and classical trivets supporting oil lamps is extremely subtle. This very refined Golden Cabinet became the loveliest of the queen's inner rooms. She met in privacy with a small coterie whom she referred to as "my society." The harp, created in 1774 by luthier Jean Henri Naderman, is a reminder that Marie-Antoinette loved to play it and received her teacher Philipp Joseph Hinner here, as well as her favorite composers and musicians, André Grétry and Gluck. If she excelled in any domain, it was music. She became a patron, protecting artists and supporting the publication of their works by Parisian houses. The private performances given in this space were a chance for her to play their works and improvise a few notes for her friends, set to the poems which had been dedicated to her. To amuse herself, the queen tried harmonizing voices, harps, and violins just for the joy of the perfect chords. For the duration of a sonata, time would stand still in the heart of the noisy palace.

113

# A BLOW
# TO THE HEART

**\* REPLICA OF THE QUEEN'S NECKLACE, BASED ON AN ENGRAVING (1963)**
QUEEN'S INNER ROOMS (3RD FLOOR)

This necklace, created in 1963 by the jeweler Burma, is a replica of the piece set with 675 sapphires which was Marie-Antoinette's misfortune. A disturbing episode in the reign of Louis XVI, the Affair of the Necklace gave rise to a resounding scandal. It all started on a summer evening in 1784, in the Grove of Venus, when the Cardinal de Rohan agreed to handle a secret transaction to buy jewelry worth 1.6 million livres on behalf of a supposed friend of Marie-Antoinette, the Countess de La Motte. After acting as a guarantor with the jewelers Bassenge et Boehmer, the cardinal gave the necklace to the countess. However, when they didn't see the queen wearing it or the first payments arriving, the jewelers went to Madame Campan, the Queen's First Lady-in-Waiting who turned them away. The affair soon became public; on August 15,

1785, when the cardinal was getting ready to celebrate Assumption Mass, Louis XVI had him arrested in the Hall of Mirrors and sent to the Bastille to be tried before the parliament in Paris. While the countess was sentenced with life imprisonment, the cardinal's acquittal was a real blow for Marie-Antoinette, who had already acquired a reputation as a spendthrift. The public quickly started blaming her for the State's bankruptcy and slapped her with the nickname "Madame Déficit." As for the famous necklace, accomplices of the countess who had fled to Switzerland and England had already dismantled it to sell the diamonds. The cardinal nevertheless had to sell his belongings to pay back the jewelers, leaving his heirs with a debt they wouldn't finish paying off until the late 19th century!

# THE QUEEN'S DAYS
## WERE NUMBERED

At dawn on October 6, 1789, the queen was awoken by a great noise under her windows. Her ladies-in-waiting, Mesdames Thibault and Augué, informed her that it was being produced by Parisian women who had come the day before to meet the king so as to obtain flour and who hadn't found a place to spend the night. Fifteen minutes later, an uproar came from the Guards' Room: rioters were forcing their way in. The ladies-in-waiting came running and, amidst of the panic, helped Marie-Antoinette to dress. Opening the little door to the left of her bed, she fled through her rooms to reach Louis XVI's bedroom. Already aware of the situation, he had come to meet the queen by another way, using an entresol corridor under the Œil-de-Bœuf Room. Seeing he had missed her, he turned back. A few minutes later, while the crowd grew in the Marble Courtyard and invaded the palace, the royal family was finally reunited in Louis XVI's bedroom. La Fayette and a few grenadiers of the National Guard had almost failed to subdue the rioters who had made it into the Œil-de-Bœuf Room.

The crowd under the windows shouted for the queen to appear on the balcony, which she did, terrified, holding the dauphin in her arms. She who had just been booed got cheers! The royals would nevertheless be forced to leave Versailles for Paris that day. During the five chaotic hours of that journey, did the queen remember June 8, 1773, and the enthusiastic applause of the crowd at her first public appearance in Paris? On that occasion, the Duke of Brissac, governor of Paris, had welcomed her with these words: "Madame, you see before you two hundred thousand people in love with you."

115

# THE PALACE'S
# LAST STEPS

**\*\*PROVENCE STAIRCASE**
SOUTH WING

This staircase—whose construction began in 1788 but was then inter-rupted—is the last of Louis XVI's architectural works in the palace; it was Louis-Philippe who finished it in the 19th century. After the royal family left Versailles on October 6, 1789, the palace was not immediately deserted. Most of the staff employed at the royal residence and the buildings and storage services kept working. They surely remembered the Regency, during which young Louis XV lived in Paris from 1715 to 1722, and thought that the situation was temporary. The installation of the National Assembly in Paris took a few days. Throughout 1790, work continued on the steps of the grand staircase in the South Wing, meant to lead to the apartments of the Count of Provence. Taking advantage of the court's absence, workers even undertook to re-gild the Hall of Mirrors! But the royal family's flight to Varennes in June, 1791 made them realize that no one was going to return. The city of Versailles, renamed "Cradle of Freedom," lost half its population as resources dried up. The palace was closed until August, 1794, when the Convention holding executive power put nearly 17,000 pieces of furniture up for sale.

# A TWENTY-MINUTE
## REIGN

**\* BATHROOM OF THE DUCHESS OF ANGOULÊME**
DAUPHINE'S APARTMENT

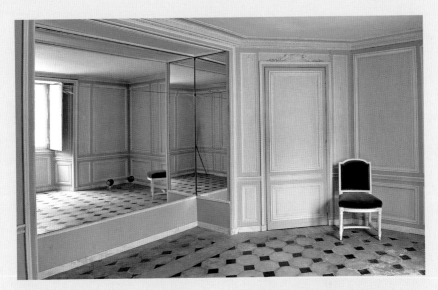

Overlooking the Queen's Courtyard, this little room was used for a while as a meridian room for the Countess of Provence before Madame Royale moved in. Under the Restoration, the apartment was once again attributed by Louis XVIII to the eldest daughter of Louis XVI and Marie-Antoinette. She asked that the former room be turned into a modern bathroom with the addition of marble flooring and a water supply. We don't know if the lone survivor of the Temple prison really enjoyed her summer stays in the palace of her childhood. Nevertheless, for Louis XVIII, she was a symbol he intended to exploit politically. Since the death of his wife in 1810, Legitimists saw her as a little queen. As the king was childless, he had her marry

Louis Antoine d'Artois, the Duke of Angoulême, the eldest son of his brother (the future Charles X). In the event of Louis XVIII's death, she would be dauphine and heir apparent to the throne; this is what happened in 1824. After the Three Glorious Days and the abdication of Charles X, we can say she reigned for twenty minutes, when the Duke of Angoulême, reluctant to sign his father's act of renunciation, was briefly Louis XIX. However, when Louis-Philippe took power, the remaining members of the Bourbon family went into exile. In 1836, upon Charles X's death, the 58-year-old duchess once again became, in the eyes of the Legitimists, the new queen. And yet she died near Vienna in 1851 without ever seeing France again.

117

# DEAD
# FOR FRANCE

## * HALL OF BATTLES
SOUTH WING (2ND FLOOR)

Five hundred and twenty eight names are engraved on the 16 bronze plaques in the Hall of Battles (1834–1837): 36 princes of the royal house, 10 admirals, 6 constables, 25 marshals, 33 warriors, 18 commanders, and 400 officers who died in combat for France. This "cathedral" devoted to the nation is a shining summary of the country's military history, from Clovis to Napoleon. However, amidst the 92 busts of great warriors and the 66 paintings depicting acts of courage and sacrifice, there is propaganda afoot. Although the Orléans are almost absent, the signature of the man who commissioned the work appears sixty times in the lunettes, in the form of the initials "LP" for Louis-Philippe d'Orléans: this omnipresence expresses the completion of the construction of national history under the aegis of the July Monarchy. The Hall finishes with the 1830 Room, devoted to the Three Glorious Days which brought Louis-Philippe to power. It showcases Eugène Devériare's painting representing the oath before the Chambers to maintain the rights acquired in the Constitutional Charter of 1814. Louis-Philippe—who styled himself king of the French, not of France— intended to peacefully rally together all the political movements arising from the Revolution, including the Legitimists. This is why he wanted to feature the names of the old aristocracy on the bronze plaques; the heroism of the past and the "great memories of our history" were to be replaced by a new political modernity.

# FANTASTICALLY GOTHIC

**\* DOOR FROM THE HOSPICE OF THE KNIGHTS OF SAINT JOHN OF JERUSALEM**
CRUSADES ROOM
NORTH WING

The sculpted cedar door as well as the bronze mortar of the Hospice of the Knights of Saint John of Jerusalem in Rhodes were given to Louis-Philippe by the Ottoman Sultan Mahmud II. To show them to their best advantage, the king asked sculptor Jean-Baptiste-Louis Plantar and architect Frédéric Nepveu to come up with a decor recalling the illustrious history of this order founded in the 11th century in the Holy Land. Between 1837 and 1839, the rooms were filled with nearly 150 paintings representing the era of the Crusades and decorated with the arms of hundreds of families descended from the illustrious knights. For this occasion, the titles of the families were barely verified, so a great many made claims to nobility.

The famous door itself was not much of a model of historical authenticity, because it dates from 1512, marked with the arms of Fabrizio del Caretto, who restored the hospice's fortifications against Suleiman II. This decor, a pastiche of Gothic style with troubadour overtones, was very fashionable in the Romantic period, and aimed to plunge visitors into the ambience of a fantastical Middle Ages.
After the Revolution turned history upside down, pillaging kings' tombs, churches, and ancient relics, this forgotten period became a focus of interest once again. Like Victor Hugo's *Notre-Dame de Paris*, the Crusades Rooms did not aim to provide a scientific reproduction, but rather to express the spirit of an idealized era.

# THE LOVELIEST
# OF ILLUSIONS

## *STAIRCASE TO THE CHIMAY ATTIC

To reach the Chimay Attic, you have to take a lovely staircase extending from the Queen's Staircase. Its decoration might lead you to believe it was created in Louis XIV's time, but it was in fact ordered by Louis-Philippe and his wife, Queen Marie-Amélie de Bourbon-Siciles. Constructed between 1833 and 1837, its extremely realistic marbles are made of stucco, a mixture of colored marble and plaster, hardened and brushed to create cracks which were then filled with a paste imitating crystals. The whole was then polished and buffed to a shine with wax-soaked woolen cloths. As for the name "Chimay," it was erroneously attributed to this attic... and it stuck! The Princess of Chimay, Laure-Auguste de Fitz-James, lady of the palace to Marie Leszczynska and lady-in-waiting to Marie-Antoinette for fourteen years, didn't really live in this part of the palace located above the queen's apartments. She only had two small rooms there, for daytime rest, whereas her splendid apartment was located in the attic of the South Wing, where there is now the glass roof of the Hall of Battles.

# AN INCONVENIENT OATH

**\* SKETCH FOR *THE TENNIS COURT OATH* (1792), BY JACQUES LOUIS DAVID**
CHIMAY ATTIC

This sketch by Jacques Louis David is just one of three remaining pieces of *The Tennis Court Oath* which the painter had tried to finance in 1790 by subscriptions from the Jacobins to commemorate this major episode in the Revolution on June 20, 1789. What we see at Versailles is the central detail presenting the outlines of a few deputies, only four of whose faces are finished: Antoine Barnave, Père Gérard, Edmond Dubois de Crancé, and the Count of Mirabeau, who had posed in the studio in the Church of the Feuillants. In 1792, the project was suspended because the subscription effort failed and the Revolution had become radicalized, which made it impossible to have moderate figures in the painting, such as Mirabeau, whose correspondence with the king had been seized when the Tuileries Palace was taken. At first, David thought he could make the oath-takers anonymous, but he ended up abandoning the project. It was not until the 2nd Republic that the original work, in poor condition and cut into three pieces, emerged from storage at the Louvre for an exhibition in the Tennis Room at Versailles on July 14, 1848. Nevertheless, the curators, finding it too indecent, chose to send it back. It was only 35 years later,

in preparation for the centennial of the French Revolution and the inauguration of the Museum of the Revolution in the Tennis Room on June 20, 1883, that a finished version was commissioned, to be created by Luc-Olivier Merson using David's sketchbooks. As for the unfinished painting, it was exhibited from 1880 onwards in the drawings room of the École Francaise du Louvre, before being transferred to the Palace of Versailles in 1921.

Museum of the Revolution,
1, Rue du Jeu-de-Paume.

# THE NAPOLEONIC
## LEGEND

**\*\* *NAPOLEON'S LAST DAYS ON SAINT HELENA* (1866), BY VINCENZO VELA**
SOUTH WING (ATTIC)

Napoleon III bought this spectacular marble from Italian sculptor Vincenzo Véla during the 1867 Universal Exhibition in Paris, with a view to installing it at the Palace of Versailles. This makes it one of the few Napoleonic works at Versailles not to be contemporary with the creation of Louis-Philippe's museum. It shows us the fallen emperor depicted in a disturbing posture of defeat and introspection: Napoleon, prisoner on Saint Helena, holds a map of Europe open on his knees and stares at the horizon. The work is the symbolic end of the 120-meter-long perspective of the

South Wing attic, where nearly 150 paintings linked to the history of the Consulate and the First Empire are presented. While Napoleon III was certainly moved by this vibrant homage to his uncle by a foreign artist, he also found in this work the exaltation of a myth on which he had founded the legitimacy of his taking power. The sculpture was an immediate success in France and throughout Europe. Copied by numerous artists and reproduced in several bronze editions by the Barbedienne house, it was among the most popular works of the late 19th century.

# THE HISTORY OF GREAT MEN

**SCULPTURES OF THE GREAT MEN OF FRANCE**
STONE HALLWAY
NORTH WING (2ND FLOOR)

The Museum of the History of France at Versailles is connected with Louis-Philippe, without any great thought for the various initiatives prior to its creation. However, among the sculptures of the Great Men of France commissioned for the four stone hallways there are also, on the second floor of the North Wing, those which were part of the Count of Angiviller's 1776 commission for the Grand Gallery of the Louvre, destined to become a museum, according to the wishes of Louis XVI. Although 27 of these sculptures of "Illustrious Frenchmen" were indeed created, the museum project lay dormant. The National Assembly relaunched it in 1791, opening the Central Arts Museum two years later. In 1797,

Versailles welcomed the Museum of the French School, exhibiting seventeenth- and eighteenth-century paintings. It did not endure, and it took until the arrival of Louis-Philippe for the palace to find a new vocation. In order to celebrate the highlights of French history and illustrious figures, some of the sculptures from the 1776 commission were transferred to the museum while the Great Men collection was filled out with copies. The space was also open to original works, such as the marble statue of Joan of Arc by Marie of Orléans, the king's second daughter, which was delivered in 1837 for the museum's inauguration and installed on the ground floor of the North Wing.

# NEVER TO BE
## FINISHED

**THE OLD WING AND THE DUFOUR PAVILION**
SOUTHERN PASSAGE TOWARDS THE GARDEN

Napoleon wanted to make Versailles into an imperial residence. He therefore took up the "Grand Design" developed by Jacques Ange Gabriel in 1747, with the idea of replacing the polychrome façades of the palace with noble limestone ones. Indeed, it was he, and not Louis XVIII, who in 1814 ordered the destruction of the foremost pavilion of the old wing which ran along the south of the Royal Courtyard and

which dated back to Louis XIV. But the fall of the regime put a halt to the project by architects Alexandre Dufour and Pierre-François-Léonard Fontaine.

Under the Restoration, Louis XVIII kept Dufour on, entrusting him with the complete rebuilding of the South Wing on the model of the Gabriel Wing on the north side of the Royal Courtyard. This task was carried out between 1772 and 1774. However, from 1820 on, the ailing invalid king did not return to Versailles, and the only work done undid Napoleon's order: the foremost pavilion was rebuilt.

Charles X, brother and successor to Louis XVIII, scarcely paid any more attention to Versailles. This is why the Dufour Pavilion remains incomplete in appearance; on the south side it jogs out from the original brick and stone façade. The grand pediment over its entrance remains empty of the sculptures planned by Louis XVIII. Louis-Philippe made do with engraving each pediment of the two pavilions with his museum's dedication: *À toutes les Gloires de la France* (To all the glories of France). Since then, while many sculptures on the façades of Versailles have been restored and replaced, no one has ever considered completing something which never was. Only the monumental staircase in the Gabriel Wing was completed in 1984, providing access to the King's Grand Apartment. It had been designed by the architect in 1752 and had awaited construction ever since.

# NO PARTIES FOR FRANCE

In the Congress Room, the traditional "RF" monograms of the French Republic (*République française*) are rather surprisingly two "F"s back to back. This unusual presentation has been explained by the conservatism which reigned upon the birth of the 3rd Republic. The monarchist parliamentary majority elected in February 1871, in session at Versailles while Paris was rocked by the Commune, was in fact preparing for the restoration of the monarchy. The uncertain future of the Republic under the provisional government of Adolphe Thiers was said to have been the reason for the imposition of the back-to-back "F"s in this way. As it happened, at the time, the parliamentarians didn't sit in this room, but in the Royal Opera at Versailles! The monogrammed room was only created in 1875 by Edmond Joly, after the constitutional laws had officially made France a parliamentary republic headed by a president elected by an absolute majority of votes in the Chambers gathered in Congress. The two "F"s couldn't, therefore, have represented the hesitancy of the regime. Until 1958, this room in the South Wing was used precisely for supreme election. One thousand five hundred parliamentarians sat there in alphabetical order, gathered to give France a head of state who would place himself above the parties. It seems that the omission of the "R" for Republic was intended to avoid any existing ambiguity with the "R" from the "Republican" party federating the forces on the left.

# THE REPUBLIC'S
## ELECTED OFFICIALS

**\*\* OFFICE OF THE PRESIDENT OF CONGRESS
OR INVESTITURE OFFICE**
PROVENCE PAVILION
SOUTH WING

This former drawing room of the Countess of Provence became, under the 4th Republic, the prestigious work room of the National Assembly's President. It had already been at the heart of history from the start of the 3rd Republic because from 1879 to 1953, fourteen French Presidents had been elected there: Jules Grévy, Sadi Carnot, Jean Casimir-Perier, Félix Faure, Émile Loubet, Armand Fallières, Raymond Poincaré, Paul Deschanel, Alexandre Millerand, Gaston Doumergue, Paul Doumer, Albert Lebrun, Vincent Auriol and René Coty. After the election of the Chambers gathered in Congress, the votes were counted in this room, then the great doors were opened to the adjoining Marengo Room, where the parliamentarians awaited the announcement of the results. To the sound of applause, the new president then climbed the monumental staircase separating him from those who elected him and solemnly received his notification. However, elections were not always easy, as evidenced by the one in 1953, when it took thirteen voting rounds for the parliamentarians to agree on the name of René Coty.

From 1958 on, the electing function of Parliament was suspended by the referendum called by General de Gaulle. This change, which preceded the 1962 adoption of direct universal suffrage, aimed at avoiding laborious elections and including citizens in this great moment in the life of the nation. From then on, parliamentarians only convened in Versailles to review the Constitution.

*Staircase of the Investiture, Marengo Room.

# LOUIS XVI RIDES ON!

## EQUESTRIAN STATUE OF LOUIS XIV (1836)
PLACE D'ARMES

This equestrian statue of Louis XIV, transported to the Place d'Armes in 2009, is composed of two elements which weren't meant to be assembled together. While Louis Petitot did indeed create this sculpture of Louis XIV in 1836, the horse is from the equestrian monument honoring Louis XVI, which his brother Louis XVIII wanted to see in the center of the current Place de la Concorde, renamed Place Louis XVI in memory of the martyred king. This statue commissioned from sculptor Pierre Cartellier was meant to replace the one of Louis XV by Edme Bouchardon, which had been toppled by the revolutionaries.

There were delays, so much so that the first stone of the pedestal was only laid by Charles X on May 3, 1826. In 1829, the horse was finally ready. Meanwhile, the overthrow of the regime put a stop to the project. Louis-Philippe did not want any monument to recall or symbolize recent history—the subject of much discord—and saw the Luxor Obelisk, a gift from the Egyptian Viceroy Mehemet Ali, the perfect monument for this "Place," upon which he bestowed the name we know today. This is when he asked sculptor Louis Petitot, son-in-law of Pierre Cartellier, who had died in 1831, to adapt the horse to a new rider to pay homage to Louis XIV, the great builder of Versailles. The statue was placed in full view in the Royal Courtyard, on the site of the gate destroyed during the Revolution. But one hundred and seventy-two years later, the restoration of the railings finally forced the statue of Louis XIV to be relocated.

LOUIS XIV

# THE DESK
## OF PEACE?

**\*\* TREATY OF VERSAILLES DESK (MID-18TH CENTURY)**
NINETEENTH-CENTURY ROOMS
NORTH WING (ATTIC)

This desk went down in history when the palace curator chose it for the signature of the treaty which ended the First World War in the Hall of Mirrors on June 28, 1919. The choice was symbolic, because it was here that Kaiser Wilhelm had proclaimed the German Empire on January 18, 1871, as the French troops were defeated. Taking revenge for the wound that Prussia had inflicted, France humiliated an already defeated nation a little bit more. Representatives from all over the world had been invited, without, of course, including any leaders of the vanquished States. While this treaty led to the creation of the League of

Nations, the tough sanctions on Germany were to have grave consequences. The same ruling was applied to the Austro-Hungarian Empire on June 4, 1920 by the Trianon Treaty signed in the Cotelle Gallery of the Grand Trianon. And yet, at the time, as indicated in tourist brochures from the 1920s, these events made Versailles a peace symbol. The later consequences of the peace treaties suggest that this end to the war wasn't the deftest of solutions. Having become an ambiguous symbol, the "desk of peace" now stands in oblivion in a corner of the Museum of the History of France.

# VERSAILLES
# THE PARK

# THE SOURCE OF A LEGEND

**\*\* GALLY FARM**
ROUTE DE BAILLY, SAINT-CYR-L'ÉCOLE
TEL: 01 30 14 60 60 - WWW.FERME.GALLY.COM

Acquired in 1684 by Louis XIV to supply the court with dairy products, the Gally Farm located at the end of the Allée de la Ceinture remains active to this day. It is one of the region's oldest buildings, founded in the 11th century by the abbots of the Abbey of Sainte-Geneviève-du-Mont in Paris to clear what is now the Plain of Versailles. It was named for the valley, the Val de Galie (now spelled "Gally"), which indicated the presence of a brook. The latter's course can be followed starting from the junction with the Grand Canal to the west, running along the Allée du Plat Fond to the little town of Rennemoulin, where it becomes a little stream, a sub-tributary of the Seine. Originally, its source was located near the palace, on the Butte de Versailles, where there was a village with a church, a mill,

and a manor house in the year 1038, according to the charter granted to Lord Hugo de Versailliis. The spelling of the name "Versailles" is connected to these brooks which ran down the small hills on the plain, as well as to the Latin root *versare*, "to turn over," which we can interpret as the act of clearing the land.

The somewhat exaggerated legend of the swamps spread by Saint-Simon was a kind of honor paid to the giant worksite undertaken here by Louis XIV. However, in the early 17th century, Versailles had already long been a prosperous region, split between pastures and the game-rich forest. Louis XIII chose this property for its hunting and the agricultural potential which were to provide food for his table.

# THE LAND OF THE GONDIS

**CRITON GATE**
AVENUE DU FORT, NOISY-LE-ROI

Before being purchased by Louis XIII, the land of Versailles belonged to the prestigious Florentine Gondi family, who arrived in Henry II's court in Catherine de' Medici's wake. In 1572, Albert de Gondi seized the lands of Martial de Loménie, Charles IX's Secretary of Finance, to build the Château de Noisy. Nothing remains of the château but the main gate, which was integrated into the wall surrounding the Grand Parc. For several months in 1607, however, the château had housed Henry IV's children during the plague epidemic afflicting Saint-Germain-en-Laye. Louis XIII went on his first hunts there with the Gondi sons, Henri and Jean-François, before establishing his hunting lodge in 1623 on the heights of Versailles, the famous little "palace of cards." In 1622, Pope Gregory XV's elevation of the diocese of Paris to the rank of archdiocese, with Jean-François de Gondi at its head, preceded Louis XIII's purchase of the seigneury in 1631.

There ensued a patient policy of extension through the purchase of neighboring land, continued by Louis XIV. The Gondis' state of grace was not to last however. Compromised during the Fronde civil war, the heir Jean-François Paul, the Cardinal of Retz, was thrown into prison in 1652. Subsequently, the Château de Noisy was owned by Jacques Bénigne Bossuet, before finally being integrated into the grounds of Versailles in 1675, along with the seigneury of Marly-le-Chastel where, in 1676, Louis XIV began building his pleasure palace, Marly. The derelict Château de Noisy was demolished in 1732.

# AT THE GATES
## OF THE ROYAL DOMAIN

**FOREST PAVILION, JOUY GATE**
RUE DU PETIT-JOUY, LES LOGES-EN-JOSAS

In 1684, the former hunting grounds were enclosed by a 43-kilometer wall, longer than the Parisian ring road! This pavilion, which was used by the royal gamekeepers, is one of the twenty-two gates in that wall. While Louis XIII had contented himself with exercising the fullness of his royal hunting rights on neighboring properties, Louis XIV became the sole owner in the region. From 1664 to 1705, he incorporated seigneuries and various fiefs into an 8,000-hectare domain made up of two parts: the 1,700-hectare Petit Parc comprising the gardens corresponding to Louis XIII's first park, the Swiss Lake, the Grand Canal, the Menagerie, and Trianon, and the Grand Parc, true hunting grounds spread over 6,000 hectares. Completed by the 2,000 hectares of the Marly estate, the size of the Grand Parc was unprecedented. The Allée de Villepreux stretched almost 5 km beyond the vista of the Grand Canal! Eight villages—excluding the destroyed Trianon—were incorporated: Bailly, Bois-d'Arcy, Buc, Guyancourt, Fontenay-le-Fleury, Noisy, Rennemoulin, and Saint-Cyr. Because their farmers supplied the grain used to raise game, the domain was broken up after Napoleon stopped hunting here. Released from their obligation, the farmers bought

back the fields they had been renting. In the kings' time, they had, however, been quite well-off, because the rents they were charged were often half the going rate, and they were paid for their harvests. Naturally, working for the royal domain of Versailles was an honor, but it was also an advantage which led to the constitution of veritable family dynasties.

# A-HUNTING
# WE WILL GO...

### SCULPTURES OF THE "CABINET OF ANIMALS OF THE SOUTH" OR FOUNTAIN OF THE DAYBREAK (1684)
TO THE LEFT OF THE WATER PARTERRE FROM THE PALACE

The *Tiger Bringing Down a Bear* and the *Bloodhound Killing a Stag*, which adorn the Fountain of the Daybreak, are allegories of the art of the hunt: the tiger represents the hunter's controlled aggression and the bloodhound his perseverance and intelligence. Created by Jacques Houzeau, they mirror the sculptures of the symmetrical Fountain of Evening, the *Lion Bringing Down a Boar* and the *Lion Bringing Down a Wolf*, by Corneille Van Clève and Jean-Melchior Raon, which symbolize the courage and strength of the hunter king. While hunting was a form of entertainment, it was also a school of endurance, a means to perfect the art of horse-riding and prepare for war. In his work *De l'instruction de monsieur le Dauphin* (On the Dauphin's Instruction, 1640), François de La Mothe Le Vayer therefore recommended this practice which makes one robust and fortifies the complexion. Like his grandfather Henry IV and his father Louis XIII, Louis XIV was most assiduous, hunting for more than one hundred days a year, and sometimes several days in a row. Hunting with hounds corresponded with the qualities esteemed by the Nobles of the Sword: courage, humility, and self-sacrifice. Additionally,

it constituted a political instrument allowing the king to show off his physical strength and war-like qualities. As on his hunts, Louis XIV particularly enjoyed siege warfare: of the forty-two campaigns led by Vauban, the king himself supervised nineteen, a fact he ably used for his propaganda. It's no coincidence that the sculptures of the two "Cabinets of Animals" were cast at the Arsenal by the Frères Keller in the same bronze as that used for the cannons of the royal army. Completed in 1684, their military ties honored the policy of uniting the foreign enclaves of northern France.

# THE VESTIGES OF THE MENAGERIE

**\*\* GATEWAY TO THE LANTERN PAVILION**
AVENUE DE LA DIVISION-LECLERC, VERSAILLES

These two terms (statues on square pillars) of stag heads are the last vestiges of the former Royal Menagerie built by Le Vau between 1662 and 1664—Louis XIV's first intervention at Versailles. In 1787, it was Louis XVI who had them transferred to the Pavilion, a hunting lodge, built for the captain of the hunt. These statues were originally part of a group of thirty-five others, men and women transformed into animals or having their attributes, which were scattered along the walls and gates of the Menagerie's court-yards. The stag heads were inspired by the hunter Acteon in Ovid's *Metamorphoses*, who after sparking the fury of Diana during a hunt, was turned into a stag, then devoured by his own dogs. Seeking their master, the dogs entered the cave of the centaur Chiron who, to console them, built them a statue of Acteon. This myth doubtless prompted the design of the Menagerie, at whose center there was a grotto with little streams of water which sprayed visitors. Around the central octagonal pavilion crowned with a lantern there were seven courtyards which held boar, deer, and pheasant—mostly wild game from the domain. While Louis XIV owned exotic birds and a few rare animals, it was mainly under Louis XV that tigers, rhinoceri, and elephants were brought to Versailles. Before becoming a zoo, the Royal

Menagerie played an educational role for the royal children. In 1698, Louis XIV put it at the disposal of his 13-year-old great-niece, Marie-Adélaïde of Savoie, who was to ensure the future of the dynasty. Remnants of the two pavilions created by Jules Hardouin-Mansart date from that period; they are the lone vestiges spared by the nineteenth-century sell-off.

** Former pavilion of the Duchess of Bourgogne at the Royal Menagerie.

# FABLES
# OF THE LABYRINTH

**\*\*SURVIVING SCULPTURES FROM THE LABYRINTH FOUNTAINS**
COLLECTION OF SEVENTEENTH-CENTURY SCULPTURES
PETITE ÉCURIE

These few polychrome lead animals are the only ones to have survived from the famous 39 fountains with 333 animals in the Grove of the Labyrinth (1660–1677), which was destroyed when the gardens were replanted under Louis XVI to make room for the current Queen's Grove. Jacques Bénigne Bossuet led the dauphin to discover them in the right order in something like a voyage of initiation, by finding the correct way along the sinuous paths. Each scene was based on one of Gabriel Faërne's *Fables* (1564)—the Latin translation of the *Fables* by the Greek writer Aesop, created following a request by Pope Pius IV—and was complemented by a maxim devised by Isaac de Benserade, poet of the court ballets. Also produced thanks to Charles Perrault,

member of the Académie Française, and the sculptors from Charles Le Brun's team, these creations aimed, through representation, to reveal the messages contained in the fables, considered useful for the education of young children since the Counter-Reformation. Charles Perrault only belatedly translated Faërne's Latin version into French (in 1699, soon after his famous fairy tales), well after Jean de La Fontaine had published a dozen volumes of his *Selected Fables* (1668–1694), dedicated to the Grand Dauphin, to Madame de Montespan, and to the Duke of Bourgogne (Louis XIV's grandson). It was nevertheless Charles Perrault who won the day at Versailles, as Louis XIV probably never forgave La Fontaine for the support he had provided Nicolas Fouquet in the past.

# FOUQUET'S
## LEGACY

**HERCULES, MINERVA, AND *FLORA* (1656)**
GIRANDOLE GROVE

Terms are the statues atop pillars which mark the edges of gardens, in reference to the Roman god Terminus who was associated with their protection. Before belonging to Louis XIV, those present in the Girandole Grove belonged to Nicolas Fouquet: *Hercules, Minerva, Flora, Harvester, Bacchus, Pomona, Vertumnus* and *Bacchante*, created in Rome in 1655 based on drawings by Nicolas Poussin. Fouquet had them installed in his Château de Vaux-le-Vicomte after paying handsomely for them. At the time, it wasn't unusual for the powerful to send their artists to Italy to copy ancient and Renaissance works. It was to that end that in 1666 Colbert created the Académie de France in Rome.
Louis XIV, a savvy collector, had these famous terms installed at Versailles.

The operation does not date back to the arrest on September 5, 1661, of Fouquet, his Superintendent of Finances, but to a purchase, in 1683, from his impecunious heirs. While Louis XIV took possession of some of Nicolas Fouquet's belongings and his team of artists gathered at Vaux-le-Vicomte—the trio of Le Vau, Le Brun, and Le Nôtre—, this was no case of theft. The superintendent's ruined family put everything they could up for auction, so a great deal of what Louis XIV acquired was obtained legally. The Marble Courtyard was thus paved with black and white tiles from Vaux-le-Vicomte which a desperate Madame Fouquet sold to the king in 1670 (exact replicas have since been restored at Vaux-le-Vicomte, in works carried out between 1978 and 1982).

# THE PYTHIAN GAMES

**DRAGON FOUNTAIN**

According to the *Homeric Hymn to Pythian Apollo* in Ovid's *Metamorphoses*, the newly born Apollo threw off his swaddling clothes and was filled with a vigor which led him, on a chariot drawn by swans sent by Jupiter, to defy the serpent Python, the terrible monster guarding the oracle at Delphi, which he killed with an arrow. This first feat of the Apollo legend is represented in the gilded bronzes of the Dragon Fountain, sculpted in 1667. The serpent, under attack by arrows shot by four *putti*, seems to vomit blood from his mouth in a dramatic burst which sends a jet of water raining back down on the pool. In ancient times, the Pythian Games involved contests for poetry, drama, and music which aimed to reward the best hymn to Apollo. The inauguration of the

fountain, on the occasion of the royal "Grand Divertissement" (literally, "great entertainment") at Versailles on July 18, 1668, echoed this tradition by celebrating the victorious return of the young Louis XIV from the War of Devolution as well as the signature of the Treaty of Aix-la-Chapelle. Held in a verdant theater, this grandiose celebration was centered on a pastoral with songs and ballets by Lully and Beauchamp, as well as Molière's comedy *Georges Dandin*, and ended with a bacchanal entitled *The Feasts of Love and Bacchus*. More than one hundred dancers, actors, and singers were on hand to charm the court and show the 2,000 guests the magnificence of the reign and the power of the king, as undeniable on the battlefield as in the arts.

# DANCING KING

This little amphitheater ensconced in greenery, with a waterfall trickling over shells from Bourbon Island and Madagascar, is as enchanting now as when it was first created. This decor was the setting for dance performances staged on summer evenings by the light of dozens of torches and flame vases. At the center of the grove there was originally a marble island surrounded by a little canal. This is where the dancers appeared, while the musicians were at the top of the semicircle. Although this grove was called the "Ballroom," no court balls were ever held there, but rather lyrical dance performances and opera-ballets created by Lully and Molière. It was inaugurated in 1683, so Louis XIV never danced there. At 45 years old, the king had already long left the stage, preferring to

leave it to the professionals who served his image just as well. Dance continued to have an important role in his life, as evidenced by the fact that he continued to assiduously attend classes given by Pierre Beauchamp and by his support for the Académie Royale de Danse, created in 1661. The art of dance had become one of the foundations of proper upbringing, ensuring perfect self-control and the prestige of elegance. Raoul-Auger Feuillet produced the first codification of classical dance with the creation of the five dance positions in *Orchesography, or the Art of Dancing by Characters and Demonstrative Figures* (1700). Since then, these terms have remained in French in ballet schools and companies the world over.

# THE ARSENAL
# OF THE GRAND CANAL

**LITTLE VENICE**
ALLÉE D'APOLLON
TEL: 01 39 53 25 69 - WWW.LAPETITEVENISE.COM

La Petite Venise restaurant, established in the former hangars of the Grand Canal bargemen.

At the edge of the Grand Canal there is a group of small houses, built in 1673 and used as housing and warehouses for the corporation of "bargemen of the Grand Canal", comprising one lieutenant, one master, one petty officer, eleven sailors, six gondoliers, and eight carpenters. The king's interest in the navy was such that this team ended up with more than 260 men, placed in 1707 under the authority of the Marquis of Langeron, named "Admiral of the Canal of Versailles" for his bravery during the Spanish War of Succession in the defense of the port of Toulon. Besides the rowboats, the gondolas presented by the Republic of Venice, and the English pleasure yachts, the ships here were part of a strategy of military and naval modernization: the *Galiote* (1669), armed with 32 little cannons, the *Grand Vaisseau* (1685), the *Dunkerquoise* (1685), the *Réale* and the *Grande Galère* (1686). All these were prototypes which the king could test himself before giving his orders to the kingdom's arsenals. With its 1.8-kilometer vista, the Grand Canal was also a sumptuous showcase presented to guests: from the Hall of Mirrors, the sight of the forest of masts must have been striking, particularly during celebrations when the ships were illuminated. There remains almost nothing of this flotilla which Louis XIV never stopped expanding, except the prow of Marie-Antoinette's boat, a gift from Calonne in 1777, a remarkable souvenir of the little "floating salons." Long forgotten in the abandoned hangars of Little Venice, it is now on view at the National Maritime Museum in Paris.

# OPEN
# THE FLOODGATES!

**BUC AQUEDUCT**
ROUTE DES ARCADES, BUC

To supply Versailles with water, between 1663 and 1688 Louis XIV's engineers laid out a vast network which extended for a radius of 30 kilometers around the palace. With its nineteen arches, the Buc Aqueduct, built between 1684 and 1686 by Thomas Gobert, is one of the remarkable remaining elements. It allowed water to be brought to the artificial ponds in the south and southwest from the Saclay Plateau by passing above the Bièvre Valley. Classified an historical monument, it is exceptional because of its nearly 580-meter length and its nearly 24-meter height. It is reminiscent of the Louveciennes Aqueduct in Marly, or the unfinished Maintenon Aqueduct on the Eure, which Louis XIV had imagined being of as more imposing than the Pont du Gard. Despite this unrealized dream, the engineers managed to move 8 million cubic meters of water thanks to 170 kilometers of channels and 40 kilometers of underground conduits.

For the Grandes Eaux fountains, supply remained nonetheless problematic: in the Grove of the Obelisk alone, water spurted 23 meters in the air! That meant the fountain-eers had to open and close the floodgates depending on how the royal cortege moved through the groves; they were thus alerted of royal movements by whistle signals. Thanks to the modernization of the circuit and the installation in 1981 of a pump under the Grand Canal, the fountains can now all play at the same time... even though this is only possible for a few hours at a time.

# THE PALACE OF WATER

**\*\* RESERVOIRS UNDER THE WATER PARTERRE**

During the few days in fall when the reservoirs of the Water Parterre are drained for maintenance, you can discover the gardens' underbelly. Supplied like the reservoir of the North Wing by the Butte de Montbauron reservoirs, they make it possible to irrigate an underground network of 30 kilometers of pipes, accessible through six galleries: through an interplay of communicating vessels, water spurts from the 50 fountains and nearly 670 water effects, following the slope of the ground to the huge open-air reservoirs of the Grand Canal, the Neptune Fountain, and the Swiss Lake. The ground under Versailles is like a massive water tower whose installation required the whole site to be overhauled and new techniques to be invented.

The greatest success of master fountaineer François Francine and André Le Nôtre was certainly to make the complexity of these workings invisible. Copious amounts of water seem to rush from the ground as though via a natural phenomenon. Around the pools of the Water Parterre, the eight recumbent statues created by the sculptors Tuby and Coysevox and the Keller foundrymen are perfect allegories of this hydraulic power. They represent the rivers of France

and their main tributaries: *The Loire and the Loiret*, *The Rhône and the Saône*, *The Seine and the Marne*, *The Garonne and the Dordogne*, bearing the agricultural attributes of the regions they cross. Water is symbolized as the essential element for fertilizing the rich lands of France; here, the land of Versailles is celebrated as the motherland *par excellence*.

** Underground gallery of the Latona Fountain's hydraulic system.

# IMPOSSIBLE
# TO BEHOLD

**DIANA AND HER NYMPHS BATHING (1668–1670), BY FRANÇOIS GIRARDON**
POOL BETWEEN THE PYRAMID FOUNTAIN AND THE ALLÉE DES MARMOUSETS

*iana and her Nymphs Bathing is* a classical composition depicting nude nymphs bathing and playing in a river. They are depicted in pairs, from left to right, at regular distances, thus giving the viewer the impression that the action is happening as we look on. The bodies are shown in a sensual, even provocative way, but the scene exudes an air of lightness and insouciance. Separated from the composition by the pool, the viewer can only admire it from afar, as if the nymphs belonged to an unattainable world. This distancing is reinforced by the water which covers the scene like a silver veil and makes these golden nudes hazy in the glimmering light. In this way, the nymphs are hidden from the viewer's gaze, like desirable and elusive objects. According to the myth described in Ovid's *Metamorphoses*, Diana and her nymphs were surprised by the hunter Acteon while they were bathing nude; as the sight of a goddess' body is forbidden to humble mortals, furious Diana chose to punish him by turning him into a stag. While the scene is underlined by a moral, its beauty leads the viewer to plunge into a fantastic universe. This work invites the viewer to delve deeper into the undergrowth through the Allée des Marmousets, to move away from the light to penetrate the magical world of the forest, peopled with nymphs and governed by Diana, goddess of wild Nature.

# THE ISLAND OF DELOS

**LATONA FOUNTAIN**

In his *Manière de montrer les jardins de Versailles* (way to view the gardens of Versailles), Louis XIV did not explain the meaning of the allegory of the Latona Fountain, created by Le Nôtre in 1666. People have often wanted to see it as an indirect reference to the Fronde civil war which had such an impact on the young king. In Ovid's *Metamorphoses*, Latona, the lover of Jupiter pursued by Jupiter's wife Juno, gave birth to Apollo and Diana on the island of Delos. She then went to Lycia, where, insulted by the local peasants, she asked the heavens to condemn them to live as frogs in a pond. Did the allegory represent Anne of Austria as a bare-breasted woman and her children, Louis XIV and Monsieur, the king's brother, transformed into Diana? It seems highly unlikely... In 1686, Jules Hardouin-Mansart had the group placed on a three-level marble pedestal and the sculpture of Latona was turned to face the Grand Canal, which changed the original meaning. Originally, Latona sat enthroned on a little rock at water level and her imploring face was strangely turned towards the spectators coming down from the terrace. She certainly wasn't addressing the heavens, but rather the visitors, whom she informed of the fantastic and enchanting nature of a garden governed by divinities. The little rock symbolized the bare, arid island of the Homeric hymns, where Latona gave birth to her children before promising that they would raise a magnificent temple and bring life there. In the reworked version, Delos, which means "the apparent," is Versailles, where a single design united Apollo and Diana, the Sun and the Moon, art and nature.

# THE BIRTH
# OF THE SEASONS

***THE ABDUCTION OF PROSERPINE BY PLUTO*** **(1677–1680), BY FRANÇOIS GIRARDON**
GROVE OF THE COLONNADE (ORIGINAL IN THE ORANGERIE)

This allegorical statue was part of the Great Commission of garden sculptures overseen by Le Brun in 1674. Inspired by Bernini's work in the Borghese Gallery in Rome, it depicts the birth of the seasons. Proserpine, daughter of Jupiter, was abducted by Pluto, god of Hell, who married her; from then on, she had to spend six months of the year in Hell and was only allowed to return to her mother Ceres, goddess of the harvest and fertility, in spring and summer. Before a permanent spot was found for it in the center of the Grove of the Colonnade in 1699, Le Brun had intended to install this statue along with three others devoted to the same theme around the pools of the Water Parterre. But Girardon's statue was the only one created, along with *The Abduction of Cybele by Saturn* by Regnaudin (now in the Louvre). Jules Hardouin-Mansart revised the program by renouncing any symbolic organization of the gardens. Girardon's work, notably, was to have had a central position in the axis of the Allée Royale, in relation with the pools of the four seasons—*Spring* or *Flora* by Tuby, *Summer* or *Ceres* by Regnaudin, *Fall* or *Bacchus* by the Marsy brothers, and *Winter* or *Saturn* by Girardon—which structure the gardens at the junctions of the side allées.

On the façade of the main building overlooking the Water Parterre, however, you can still see the allegorical organization intended by Le Brun, establishing the gardens on the theme of time and the seasons: on the ground floor, there are twenty-three mascarons of the *Ages of Life*, going from childhood to old age, as well as, on the attic, twelve statues representing the twelve months of the year on either side of Apollo and Diana presiding over the cycles of life.

# LITERARY
# INSPIRATION

**GROVE OF THE COLONNADE**

This ring of arcades formed by thirty-two pink and white marble Ionic columns, sheltering fountain pools, was created between 1684 and 1688, on the site of the former Grove of Springs designed by Le Nôtre which once traced a sinuous path through the woods. In 1681, 35-year-old Jules Hardouin-Mansart was named First Architect to the King, confirming his rapid ascension, while the elderly Le Nôtre, at 71, was only left with Louis XIV's friendship. The transformation of his grove into a lovely piece of architecture angered the gardener, who said to the king: "Sire, what would you like me to say? You've made a gardener of a mason, and he's given you a dish from his trade." The architect was indeed responsible for the full monumental dimension of Versailles: the Grande and Petite Écuries, the new Orangerie,

the Grand Trianon, the construction of the North and South Wings... The Grove of the Colonnade was part of this vast change in which classicism reigned, evoking the splendor of the Canopus portico, the pool at Hadrian's imperial villa in Tivoli. That said, Jules Hardouin-Mansart never went to Italy. He found his inspiration in books, notably in *Poliphilo's Strife of Love in a Dream* (1499) by Francesco Colonna, an illustrated novel of initiation relating the journey of a young hero in love, searching for the nymph Polia on the island of Venus. This garden of love crawls with references to ancient monuments, most of them immense—pyramids, temples, fountains...—, which served as models setting the tone of an ideal earthly paradise for Versailles.

# THE EMPEROR
# AND THE CONSTABLE

**\* STATUE OF LOUIS XIV AS AN *IMPERATOR* (1686), BY MARTIN DESJARDINS**
ORANGERIE

This marble statue by sculptor Martin Desjardins was commissioned by Marshal de La Feuillade to decorate the Place des Victoires in Paris, paid for by Jules Hardouin-Mansart in 1686. La Feuillade however then asked Desjardins to create a second model "cast in bronze," which was to be the one on the Place, while the marble version was given to the king. The bronze did not survive the torments of history, because in 1792, the revolutionaries melted it to make cannons. In the Louvre, you can still admire the titanic *Seated Captives* which adorned its base, depicting the vanquished nations at the Peace of Nijmegen in 1678. From 1684 to 1686 Jules Hardouin-Mansart worked on creating the new Orangerie in Versailles (to replace the small one built by Le Vau in 1663); this was found to be the perfect place to exhibit the marble. It was indeed a beautiful setting for a statue singing the praises of the monarchy's military glory, which architect Jacques François Blondel said was "worthy of the magnificence of the Romans." Its vaulted gallery, 156 meters long and 21 meters wide, is a masterpiece of stereotomy (the art of cutting and assembling stones without mortar) which sheltered the most extraordinary botanical collection of all time: more than 2,000 boxes of lemon trees, pomegranate trees, oleanders, and orange trees from Portugal, Spain, Italy, and the Sublime Door (Ottoman Empire). This treasure was preserved without heating during the winter, thanks to double glazing and five-meter-thick walls! This was necessary to provide warmth for the famous "Constable" orange tree from Pamplona, planted in 1421.

# SAVED FOR POSTERITY

This monolithic pool cut from a block of Rance marble was commissioned by Louis XIV in 1674. Octagonal in shape, it is more than three meters wide and over one meter deep, and said to have been used as a bath, even if it is more likely to have been a footbath for the king's returns from the hunt. It would have been impossible to heat so much water in marble. For a long time, this pool was nonetheless on the ground floor of the palace, in what was then the Apartment of Baths, and later the apartment where Louis XV housed his daughters. Before they were covered with wooden panels, the walls had been covered with rare marbles and decorated with columns and statues. Besides this pool, nothing of the Apartment of Baths survived, except the interior shutters of the two windows in Madame Victoire's second antechamber, which depicted sculpted basins with spurting water, dolphins, and marine attributes. The destruction of this place, which was comparable to the Grand Apartment in its luxury, began in the 1680s, when the apartment was attributed to the Marquise of Montespan, a fallen mistress. For the Count of Toulouse, the legitimate son who lived near her, the pool was covered with a floor which served as a platform for the bed. In 1750, the pool was finally moved to the gardens of the Hermitage, a property belonging to Madame de Pompadour, to be used as a pleasure pool. Sold in the 19th century, it was later found in a home in Neuilly, then at the Pink Palace in Le Vésinet. In 1934, the curator of the Palace of Versailles purchased it to place it in the Orangerie, the only site able to hold such a pool.

# A STATUE
# FOR THE AGES

**EQUESTRIAN STATUE OF LOUIS XIV (1665–1673), BY LE BERNIN**
ORANGERIE

B etter known through its replica in front of the Louvre Pyramid, Bernini's equestrian statue of Louis XIV returned to the Orangerie at Versailles in 1974. Since 1685 it had been at the far end of the Swiss Lake (where another copy has stood since 1990). Had it been exiled to the end of this vast artificial lake in order to conceal it? Louis XIV never hid the fact that

he did not appreciate the work, even if he did not dare destroy it. In 1665, during his stay in France, Bernini had promised him an equestrian effigy in the manner of the statue of Emperor Constantine he had created for the pope. However, the work was only delivered twenty years later, five years after the artist's death. In 1685, when Louis XIV laid eyes on the sculpture presented to him in the Orangerie, according to the memorialist Dangeau, he "resolved not only to remove it, but even to destroy it." The fiery Italian master's style depicted the king in a strange posture which shocked people. Louis XIV entrusted François Girardon with the task of masking the rider's identity, turning him into a Roman hero, *Marcus Curtius Sacrificing Himself in the Flames*. The statue was then placed at the end of the nearly 600-meter-long vista of the Swiss Lake, and not at the planned site—in plain view near the Neptune Fountain—where Domenico Guidi's *Renown Writing the King's History in a Book Held by Time* was installed instead. As representations of the king were destroyed during the Revolution, the portrait of Louis XIV on this last sculpture is a restoration. However, it seems that Girardon so deftly camouflaged the king's face on Bernini's equestrian statue that no revolutionary even considered destroying it. In this way, Louis XIV's anger saved a work which was long forgotten in a site chosen precisely to this end.

*Renown* (1680–1685), Neptune Fountain, by Domenico Guidi.

# THE BURNING GROVE

**FOUNTAIN IN THE GROVE OF ENCELADUS (1675–1677)**

This fountain, depicting a giant half-buried in rocks representing burning lava from a volcano, illustrates a famous mythological scene described in Ovid's *Metamorphoses*: the struggle between the Giants and the gods following the first defeat of the Titans. The goddess of the Earth, in an attempt to take revenge on Jupiter, sent her sons, the Giants, to fight and invade Mount Olympus. Having deserted the battlefield, one of them, Enceladus, was pursued by Minerva, daughter of Jupiter, goddess of War and the Arts, who crushed him on what is now Sicily and buried him alive under Mount Etna. Its eruptions are said to be his roars, its tremors the result of his thrashing. At Versailles, the story of Enceladus reflects the stakes in the Dutch War which saw the Most Christian King set

out to punish the Protestant Republic. The 1675 commission for the sculpture took place during the first European Grand Alliance, established in 1673 in The Hague to counter the French policy of aggression and expansion into the Spanish Netherlands. Here, as Holland is embodied by Enceladus, the attacked have become the attackers. This work of propaganda aimed to rally opinion and the nobility behind Louis XIV, who was diplomatically isolated and engaged in a European war. Inaugurated during the summer of 1677, while decisive battles seemed to be giving the French the upper hand, the Grove of Enceladus was a genuine political symbol. In this conflict which had already lasted five years, a victorious conclusion was seen as inevitable.

# THE REMAINS
## OF TRIUMPH

### *FRANCE TRIUMPHANT* (1683)
GROVE OF THE ARC DE TRIOMPHE

Until quite recently, this grove was in ruins, overwhelmed by vegetation. It features a remarkable sculpture, which has been restored and regilded and was once accompanied by magnificent wrought objects dating from 1683: a huge triumphal arch—a triple-arched gilded lead fountain—and two other fountains entitled *Glory* and *Victory*. *France Triumphant* reflects the past splendor of this "verdant room" without equal in the gardens. Appearing as Minerva on a chariot, coiffed with a helmet adorned with a rooster and armed with a fleur-de-lys lance and a shield decorated with a sun, France dictates her law to Europe. At her feet, the countries vanquished by the Peace of Nijmegen in 1678 are represented as captives: Spain is leaning against a roaring lion that is lying down, and Austria is leaning against a dying eagle, while helmets lie on the ground. On the marble steps of the fountain, there is also an expiring hydra and a many-headed dragon symbolizing the disunity of the Grand Alliance created in 1673. However, this triumph was soon to be tarnished by new conflicts largely due to Louis XIV's ongoing policy of aggression in peacetime. Furthermore, the revocation of the Edict of Nantes in 1685 led to the formation, in 1686, of a new and formidable European coalition, the League of Augsburg. There followed nine more years of a conflict which bled France dry. All precious metals were taken to finance the war machine; thankfully, the sculpture of *France Triumphant* was not made of solid gold!

# FROM THE MIND
# OF THE KING

**GROVE OF THE THREE FOUNTAINS**

Plans, engravings, and paintings helped the 2005 restoration of the Grove of the Three Fountains to a state close to that in which Le Nôtre left it in 1679. This grove is composed of three terraces that broaden at the base and alternate with flat pools and rock pools with waterfalls. The largest of these pools is made up of a huge lead and steel shell four meters in diameter. A dig also unearthed the stone ramp installed in the early 18th century to allow an aging Louis XIV to get around on wheels. The slopes of the grove now once again have the grassy steps in Le Nôtre's original design. The originality of this grove lies more specifically in the enchanting jets of water which form a magnificent three-part composition: those in the lower pool make a fleur-de-lys shape,

those in the middle pool form vertical lances and a vault of water, and those in the upper pool make an imposing column of water. It is a wonderful illustration of the inventiveness employed by Le Nôtre and master fountaineer François Francine to entertain and charm the senses. Louis XIV constantly participated in this adventure, often directing installations himself. During his military campaigns and trips, he regularly requested news of his groves, and sometimes even took up tools like a real gardener. He actively participated in the creation of the Grove of the Three Fountains, the only garden mentioned as being "from the mind of the king".

# A FRANCE FOR CHILDREN

Six children play with flowers on a rock while two others play in the water. Dating from the 1710s, the work by Jean Hardy illustrates the elderly Louis XIV's taste for celebrating childhood. We know the instructions given to Jules Hardouin-Mansart on September 10, 1699 for the interior decoration of the pavilions of the Duchess of Bourgogne at the Menagerie: "It seems to me something needs to be changed... Childhood must be spread everywhere."

In the early 18th century, Louis XIV was seen as an old man in a France where it was rare to live past 60. The bitterness of his decline was further heightened by a series of deaths in the royal family; in 1714, the king's numerous descendants had dwindled to one child. During this dark period, the glorifica-

tion of youth served the legend of Versailles as a paradise by exalting the beauty and magic of life. It also expressed Louis XIV's genuine interest in children and their education: with Madame de Maintenon, the king turned teacher and was a remarkable grandfather, giving in to the pleasure of of "coddling" while preparing his succession. However, the childhood he desired to be represented everywhere was mainly going to be that of the new France which was stirring at the end of the longest reign the country had ever known.

# THE MORGANATIC QUEEN

**\*\* NOTRE-DAME CHAPEL, SAINT-CYR SPECIAL MILITARY SCHOOL**
2, AVENUE JEAN-JAURÈS, SAINT-CYR-L'ÉCOLE

In 1684, Madame de Maintenon created the Maison Royale de Saint-Louis, a boarding school for the daughters of impoverished nobility. She herself came from a noble but ruined Protestant family; born in a prison in Niort, as a young girl she had only ever experienced a strict convent education. Her institution, also desired by Louis XIV, was, on the contrary, open to the world, to arts and letters. As she put it, Saint-Cyr was the child they couldn't have. It was natural that her remains were placed there in 1719, under the nave of Notre-Dame Chapel. However, in 1794, revolutionaries desecrated her tomb. In 1836, in a recess of the chapel's choir, a black marble mausoleum was built by way of reparation. The latter was destroyed in 1890 to punish the woman who was accused of having caused the revocation of the Edict of Nantes. A few decades later, in 1944, when German-occupied Saint-Cyr was bombarded, an old chest was discovered in the rubble. It contained the noble remains, although no one knows how these ended up there! As a final honor, the remains of Madame de Maintenon were placed in the Royal Chapel of the Palace of Versailles before being returned to the chapel of Saint-Cyr in 1969; she now rests there under a marble slab in the central aisle. The morganatic wife of Louis XIV is still the only member of the royal family to be buried in the very ground of Versailles.

# THE LAST BOLTS
# OF NEPTUNE

***NEPTUNE AND AMPHITRITE* (1736–1740)**
NEPTUNE FOUNTAIN

I n 1736, an old project by Le Brun for the semicircular lake beside the Dragon Fountain was rekindled and *Neptune and Amphitrite* was placed on a huge seashell used as a chariot, surrounded by *Proteus and a Marine Unicorn* and *The Ocean Leading a Marine Herd*, accompanied in each upper corner of the fountain by a *Marine Dragon Led by a Cherub*. This superb composition, which mobilized many sculptors under the direction of Jacques Ange Gabriel, was greatly admired. The height and variety of its 99 sprays of water outdid all the other works in the gardens. As fate would have it, however, this ensemble glorifying the sea foreshadowed a major military turning point in France's maritime destiny. The calamitous Treaty of Aix-la-

Chapelle in 1748 failed to resolve the colonial rivalries between France and England, and the tensions soon sparked a second conflict, the Seven Years' War. In 1763, The Treaty of Paris decapitated the patiently built French colonial empire, to the advantage of the English. France lost Canada, the territories of eastern Mississippi, most of the Sugar Islands, with the exception of Guadeloupe, Marie-Galante, and Sainte-Lucie, and especially its positions in India, retaining just five trading posts—Pondichéry, Karikal, Yanaon, Mahé, and Chandernagor—, and was forbidden from stationing an army there. This invocation of the gods of the sea, Louis XV's only work in the gardens of Versailles, can hardly be said to have brought luck to the reign.

# WINTER
## THRILLS AND SPILLS

**\*\* *LEOPARD SLEIGH (1730)***
COACH GALLERY
GRANDE ÉCURIE
1, AVENUE ROCKEFELLER
INFORMATION AT THE PALACE OF VERSAILLES

Of the hundreds of sleighs in the royal collection, only ten were preserved after the revolutionary sell-off. These fantastic vehicles in pasteboard and rare woods, created by the Menus-Plaisirs, varied decoration inspired by aquatic, animal, or winter themes. However, none remain from the time of Marie-Antoinette, whom we know had a great passion for races on these vehicles. In January 1774, Louis XV wrote: "Madame la Dauphine was only out once on a sleigh; Friday, the snow melted, to her great regret." Other accounts, such as those of Madame Campan or the Marquis of Dangeau, evoke these moments of escape which were already all the rage under Louis XIV.

The memorialist tells of a day when the ice on the Grand Canal was too thin, and the dauphin "was up to his neck in the water, and the princesses were tipped over."
The effects of theLittle Ice Age and its polar temperatures were nonetheless merciless in the early 18th century: in the winter of 1709, wine even froze in glasses. In 1693 and 1694, nearly 2 million French people died of cold. These extreme climatic phenomena gradually became less frequent, but on the eve of the Revolution, there were still terrible weeks during which human and agricultural activities were paralyzed and the poorest were hard-hit.

# BY THE POWER OF HERCULES

**SAINT-ANTOINE GATE**

The construction of this monumental gate was ordered in 1786 to replace the old Saint-Antoine Gate which opened the Petit Parc to the village of Le Chesnay and the road to Marly. Contemporary with the Queen's Hamlet at the Petit Trianon, it accompanied the replanting of the gardens decided by Louis XVI in 1775. Up until 1784, Versailles once again looked like the worksite the Marquise of Sévigné had known in the 17th century, marked by to-ings and fro-ings of the dense forests brought from Normandy, Flanders, and the Dauphiné. In his vast projects, Louis XVI even envisaged resuming work on the Eure Aqueduct in Maintenon and launched a consultation in 1786 to complete the Grand Design of the city side of the palace. The allegory on the keystone of the triumphal arch of the Saint-Antoine Gate is not unrelated to this ambition. It features the carcass of the Nemean lion with its impenetrable fur, killed by Hercules with a club during the first of his twelve labors. The lion skin, a primordial attribute and emblem of strength, was represented here by Joseph Deschamps. In Versailles, the major works succeed and echo each other. The allegory of Hercules cloaked with the lion skin can also be seen in other parts of the grounds—in the Royal Courtyard, for example, among the sculptures created in 1682 on the arcade keystones and the balcony supports which surround the passages leading to the gardens. Here, the Hercules allusion symbolically marks the entrance into a world where nature has been tamed and magnified by royal hands.

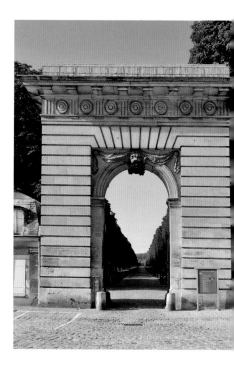

# A PLACE FOR
# THE SUN TO REST

**GROVE OF APOLLO'S BATHS**

Among the changes ordered by Louis XVI as part of the replanting of the gardens, the Grove of Apollo's Baths by Jules Hardouin-Mansart underwent major alterations. The gilded-lead daises created in 1704, which protected the three surviving groups of marble sculptures from the former Grotto of Tethys (1666), were in very poor condition. The fashion in landscaped gardens tended to the natural and picturesque, so in 1778, painter Hubert Robert proposed to create a new kind of scenography for Versailles. The sculptures would be placed in a few recesses in a cliff evoking ancient ruins, with waterfalls spilling into a pool. This composition was in keeping with the allegorical meaning of the sculptures depicting Apollo who, after driving the chariot of the sun, ended his glorious race through the heavens by descending into the waves of the goddess Tethys to relax. Hubert Robert renewed the coherence of the works of Girardon, Regnaudin, Tuby, Marsy, and Guérin: *Apollo Tended by the Nymphs* and *Tritons Grooming Two Horses of the Sun.* Perhaps more than any other, his grove plunges us into the magic of Ovid's *Metamorphoses,* the major reference text translated into French for the first time in 1614 by the erudite Nicolas Renouard and which nourished Louis XIV's childhood before inspiring his gardens at Versailles.

* Tethys, "daughter of Gaia and Uranus, wife of Oceanus, mother of three thousand Oceanids and as many rivers" (Ovid, *The Metamorphoses,* book II, lines 63-100). Not to be confused with Thetis, mother of Achilles and one of the Nereids.

# A LITTLE
# DUTCH JEWEL

**EARTHENWARE TILES FROM THE PORCELAIN TRIANON**
LAMBINET MUSEUM
54, BOULEVARD DE LA REINE
TEL: 01 39 50 30 32 - WWW.VERSAILLES-TOURISME.COM

Well before the installation of court, Louis XIV had wanted to create a pavilion for light meals in the Petit Parc, a sort of garden house for the most exceptional floral collection of the day. Using plans by Le Vau, between the winter of 1669 and the spring of 1670, François d'Orbay created a pavilion covered with porcelain and including parterres maintained by gardener Michel II Le Bouteux, grand-nephew by marriage to André Le Nôtre. A flower expert, he developed the practice of growing flowers in pots which he planted directly in the ground so as to be able to change color arrangements very easily every day. Two million pots were available all year round. For Louis XIV, this was also a political affair, because he sought to compete with the Dutch monopoly and know-how. Indeed, most of the bulbs from this first garden were imported from the Netherlands and the first Porcelain Trianon was decorated with earthenware from Delft. On the eve of the Dutch War, the young Louis XIV was intensely focused on the rich merchant cities of the United Provinces. This fragile pavilion did not withstand frost and soon fell into disrepair. Due to changing tastes, Louis XIV decided to demolish it in 1684 to create the marble Trianon we know today as the Grand Trianon, whose gardens, paintings, and interior woodwork still celebrate the beauty of flowers.

# THE KING'S
# RETREAT
**KING'S MUSIC ROOM**
GRAND TRIANON, NORTH WING

The shutters you see above the doors of the Music Room hide the galleries where musicians played during the king's supper. They were reached from the adjoining Round Room in which a woodwork drum to the right of the fireplace still conceals the stairs. For Louis XIV, it was a pleasant way of dining in private, with the shutters open or closed—either way, he could hear the instruments. Although the king invited a select few to the Trianon, he enjoyed family meals much more, in a pleasure residence set up for his children and grandchildren to stay. When the monarch invited someone, the announcement was made to the lucky few through public lists, or the king simply spoke to them directly during a walk. The Grand Trianon was in fact open to court during the day, but no one except the king, his loved ones, and his guests were allowed to dine or sleep there. The Trianon, like Marly which was built slightly earlier, is evidence of Louis XIV's gradual retreat from the always-teeming palace. At the end of his reign, he himself disrupted the daily mechanics of the etiquette he had imposed in court, sometimes spending more than a third of the year away from the palace in the Trianon or Marly. While his successors also enjoyed private retreats, Louis XIV was the one to start this trend.

# FRENCH
# TRENCHES

**ALLÉE DES HÂ-HÂ**
GRAND TRIANON, WESTERN EXTREMITY OF THE PARK

As private as he was, Louis XIV didn't aspire to live shut up within four walls at Trianon. Separate from the grounds of Versailles, Trianon Park only covered 23 hectares! The king asked Jules Hardouin-Mansart to come up with solutions to distract riders from the impression of confinement to a small space during horseback rides. The architect turned his hand to landscaping, creating wide *allées* and complementing the forest with clearings dubbed "verdant rooms"—(Atalanta, Porticos, Vases, Boules d'Ormes, Diana, Mercury, Emperors', Six Figures...)—, which one could enter on horseback. Finally, to enhance the effect of depth, Hardouin-Mansart opened certain parts of the surrounding wall with trenches (*hâ-hâ*) which did not break the visual continuity of the vistas while preventing intrusions. It may well be the surprised exclamations of those who encountered these stealthy protective elements which gave them their colorful name. People are often too quick to attribute this invention to the art of English gardens, particularly to Charles Bridgeman's early eighteenth-century experiments, described in 1780 in Horace Walpole's *Essay on Modern Gardening*. Credit is due instead to the inventiveness of the landscape architects of Versailles led by Jules Hardouin-Mansart and the treatise of Antoine Joseph Dezallier d'Argenville, *The Theory and Practice of Gardening*, published in 1709, which was the first to describe these elements.

# RE-EMERGING
## WATERS

**WATER BUFFET (1703)**
GRAND TRIANON

Atop the Water Buffet created in 1703, the sculptures, which were originally gilded, are identified as the spouses Poseidon and Amphitrite because of the tritons in the bas-relief. And yet, Poseidon, god of the seas, rivers, and springs, had multiple feminine conquests often confused with his official wife represented in a marine cortege. Here, the bas-relief notwithstanding, it is Amomyne, rather than Amphitrite, whom Poseidon is showing how, by tipping the basin of water, he manages to create fertility on Earth. According to the myth, she is one of the fifty Danaids, daughters of King Danaos, who had to find a spring so as to save Argos from drought. During her journey, she was saved from being raped by a satyr thanks to the god who, uniting with her in love, showed her the springs which would save the city. So the Poseidon depicted atop this waterfall is a benevolent one, ordering the waters to spread over stepped basins. Jules Hardouin-Mansart was suggesting the resurgence of natural bodies of water: doubtless inspired by the waterfall re-emergences of the Lison or the Loue, tributaries of the Doubs, he used mythology to celebrate the Franche-Comté's attachment to the kingdom. Poseidon is thus the magnanimous king, concerned with his new subjects' well-being and prosperity. The lions which accompany this scene are another reference to the arms of this former Spanish province, in which this animal is associated with *billettes* (little rectangles), symbols of its forest character.

# GARDEN
## PORTRAITS

**COTELLE GALLERY**
GRAND TRIANON, NORTH WING

Louis XIV knew his gardens' equilibrium was fragile and required constant maintenance. The shrubs had to be trimmed every season, the fountains cleaned and regilded, and their piping repaired after the frost... So, in 1688, the king had the idea of passing on the legacy of the magnificence of his groves by commissioning twenty-five paintings measuring 1.39 by 2 meters. These are on exhibit in the Cotelle Gallery, named for the artist Jean Cotelle the Younger (not to be confused with Jean Cotelle the Elder, deceased in 1676), the king's portrait and miniature artist, who created twenty-one of them. Depicting long-lost groves, they have great historical importance: the Labyrinth Grove, the Grove of the Arc de Triomphe, the Water Theater, or the Marais de Madame de

Montespan, famous for its cast-iron oak whose branches sprayed water. Nonetheless, all of these historically precious paintings were almost lost. These compositions rife with nymphs and *putti* were unbearable to Napoleon... who luckily did not have the time to replace them with paintings to his glory. Reinstalled in Versailles by Louis-Philippe, it was not until 1913 that the paintings were returned to the gallery chosen by Louis XIV to honor the memory of François Francine. This commission in fact followed the death on October 24, 1688 of the master fountaineer who, along with André Le Nôtre, was the main creator of the gardens of Versailles.

# THE END
## OF A FASHION

**CHILD WITH A QUIVER (1672–1673)**
GRAND TRIANON, GARDEN

Next to the former King's Garden, behind the North Wing, there is a remarkable example of Versailles Baroque in the form of a stepped fountain of shell-encrusted basins, topped with a cherub holding a bow, taking an arrow from his quiver, and riding a dolphin. Created by Gaspard Marsy, this fountain is the last remnant in France of the Water Theater, one of the most famous groves in the gardens of Louis XIV, created by André Le Nôtre between 1671 and 1673. You'd have to go to Washington's National Gallery to admire two other elements from this grove, *Cherubs Playing with a Lyre* by Pierre Le Gros, and *Cherubs Playing with a Swan* by Baptiste Tuby. The fountain with the *Child with a Quiver* is located on the site of another lost masterpiece, the Grove of Springs, which Louis XIV had had moved from the garden of the marble Trianon during the creation of the Grove of the Colonnade in 1684. Despite abandoning his initial love of Baroque, Louis XIV retained a certain nostalgia and respect for the works of Le Nôtre.

Louis XVI, faced with the astronomical cost of their maintenance and their state of disrepair, chose to get rid of such elements as the famous Labyrinth, which was replaced by an arboretum. These demolitions also reflected changing tastes: while the Queen's Grove, with its exotic species— Virginia tulip trees, Corsican pines, Lebanese cedars, and red gum trees— retained the imagery of the pedagogical labyrinth by Le Nôtre and Charles Perrault, it placed sculpted fountains firmly in the past; they were seen as superfluous in the new art of the garden in the late 18th century.

# THE EMPEROR'S FLOWERS

**\* THE EMPEROR'S BEDROOM**
EMPEROR'S SMALL APARTMENT
GRAND TRIANON, NORTH WING

Chair in the Emperor's private cabinet.

Napoleon's private apartment in the Grand Trianon is in a part which is almost hidden from visitors. Located on the inside façade of the North Wing and symmetrical with the official rooms, it is an enfilade of five rooms with lowered ceilings: antechamber, private cabinet, bathroom, bedroom, and the Salon du Déjeun, where the Emperor took his breakfasts. He only really occupied these private, refined spaces—created from 1805 to 1807 by the best artists in his employ (Percier, Fontaine, Jacob Frères, Desmalter...)—in 1809, when he divorced Joséphine de Beauharnais. The embroidered moiré wall hangings with lemonwood work, which the Empress had ordered in 1807, remained in place.

The Emperor also made do with the early Louis XV woodwork, although he hated Rococo. As he saw it, he would only be in the Grand Trianon temporarily: he was aiming for the Palace of Versailles. On July 12, 1811, from Grand Trianon, he asked that the palace be refurnished and restored to receive the imperial family and its court. However, the abdication at Fontainebleau in 1814 stopped any projects. The Grand Trianon would remain composite, with Empire furniture side by side the natural floral decors of the 18th century. The Emperor's private cabinet, completed in 1812, was the only room fully decorated according to his tastes, with geometric floral motifs of fritillaries, his favorite flowers.

# ALL IN
## THE FAMILY

**EMPRESS MARIE-LOUISE'S BOUDOIR**
GRAND TRIANON, SOUTH WING

n 1805, Napoleon had established an apartment in the Grand Trianon for his mother, but she preferred her Château de Pont-sur-Seine. So, in 1810, he gave the rooms to his wife Marie-Louise, forcing her to live with furniture she had not chosen, illustrating the attention the Emperor paid the Archduchess of Austria upon her arrival. Marie-Louise, grand-niece of Marie-Antoinette, was in fact traded after Wagram's victory over Austria to ensure the dynastic descendants which the sterile Joséphine de Beauharnais had been unable to give the Emperor. During her four years in France, Marie-Louise had no time to impose her personality through artistic choices. The furniture in her boudoir in the Grand Trianon, although seemingly a touching testimonial at first glance, was in fact second-hand. The "triumphal arch" desk (1796) belonged to her husband and former wife from the time they lived in Paris. The high-backed couch, the two wing chairs, the four chairs, the screen, and the two footstools were the ensemble commissioned for Napoleon's sister, Pauline Borghese, from cabinetmaker François Jacob-Desmalter for her boudoir in the Petit Trianon. Taking a dim view of her brother's remarriage to an 18-year-old princess, Pauline took umbrage and left the Petit Trianon. Her furniture was moved and upholstered with new apricot silks by Darrac in 1810. For Marie-Louise, the Empire style was emblematic of a country she had

learned to hate. The "Austrian belly" was nonetheless among those faithful to Napoleon, even siding with him against her own father, although her love for her son, the King of Rome, born in 1811, was surely not unrelated to her taking that stance in the family dilemma.

# STONES
# FROM SIBERIA

**MALACHITE BASIN (1807–1809)**
MALACHITE ROOM
GRAND TRIANON, NORTH WING

This big malachite basin was a present from Czar Alexander I to Napoleon, on the occasion of the Treaty of Tilsit in 1807. It was a priceless gift, because malachite is a fragile, brilliant, intensely green stone, the only known deposit of which was in Siberia. The basin was made from hundreds of stones set in a mosaic. To set them, the Russians had invented a stone-cutting technique involving bonding together fine, millimeters-thick layers of stone before polishing. This is why Napoleon's best artists worked to show this basin to its best advantage: in 1809, François Jacob-Desmalter and Charles Percier mounted it on three large gilded-bronze chimeras in the purest Empire style. Since Antiquity, basins had been sacred objects; the chimeras with the feet of lions and the head of Hercules honored the Emperor at the height of his glory. The Treaty of Tilsit committed Alexander I to supporting Napoleon in his fight against England. The basin was therefore presented as a symbol of an allegiance that seemed to definitely sealing imperial peace on the continent. And yet, a completely different reality came to light in 1812, when the czar turned on France. This about-face led the Grand Army to the Berezina River. In 1814, the czar entered Paris at the head of European coalition troops and restored the Bourbon monarchy in favor of Louis XVIII, who dubbed him a Knight of the Holy Spirit.

# THE BOURBONS'
## LAST GASP

**BED IN THE EMPRESS' BEDROOM (1809)**
GRAND TRIANON, SOUTH WING

ouis-Philippe brought this bed from the Tuileries, where it had been since 1809, making some modifications, including the addition of his "LP" monogram in the tondo. The bed had been commissioned by Napoleon before Louis XVIII's death on September 16, 1824. Louis-Philippe was determined to claim it, doubtless because he wanted to underline the blood ties linking the royal couple to the illustrious owners of the bed—it had come to symbolize the legitimacy of the Orléans dynastic line. Louis-Philippe, son of "Philippe Égalité" who in 1793 had voted for Louis XVI's death, was the direct descendant of Louis XIV's younger brother, while his wife Marie-Amélie de Bourbon-Siciles was Louis XVI's niece,

and cousin to both Louis XVII and Empress Marie-Louise. Through this marriage, the July Monarchy aspired to embody a synthesis of the history of France. Louis-Philippe had ascended to the throne in a unique context after the revolution of the Three Glorious Days, as a replacement for Louis-Antoine d'Artois, the Duke of Angoulême, who, under the name Louis XIX, had reigned for twenty minutes, the span of time during which he hesitated to sign his father Charles X's act of abdication. It was in the Emperor's Council Room in the North Wing of the Grand Trianon that the king took his leave of his ministers on July 31, 1830, after he had failed to re-establish absolutism.

# A PRESIDENT
# IN THE PALACE

**\*\* OFFICE OF GENERAL DE GAULLE**
PRESIDENTIAL APARTMENT
GRAND TRIANON, TRIANON-SOUS-BOIS WING

A t the northern end of the Grand Trianon there is a part of the palace virtually unknown to the public: the Presidential Apartment, first renovated in 1962. Since Napoleon III's departure, the Grand Trianon had become very rundown. General de Gaulle decided to entrust the task of bringing it back to life to Culture Minister André Malraux as well as one of the top experts on the First Empire, Gérald van der Kemp. The Trianon-sous-Bois Wing was given to the head of State, who promised to put the rest of the palace at the disposal of the public when it wasn't being used for receptions and visits by foreign heads of State. The most illustrious guests were, in 1972, the Queen of the United Kingdom and the Common-wealth, Elizabeth II; in 1973, the General Secretary of the Soviet Communist Party Leonid Brezhnev; in 1978 and 1982, US Presidents Jimmy Carter and Ronald Reagan; and in 1996, Russian President Boris Yeltsin. This function was however suspended on March 26, 1999 by then President Jacques Chirac, who reincorporated the Grand Trianon into the national grounds of the Palaceof Versailles, giving it back its full role as a museum.

# A TASTE FOR SNOW

At the rear of the garden of the Petit Trianon, near the Lac du Trèfle, there are the ice houses which Louis XIV had installed in 1686 and which were in use until 1909. These little rustic buildings with thick stone walls and thatched roofs are the visible part of an installation anchored deeply in the ground in order to maintain a constant temperature below 0 °C. One entered through a two-door airlock, the second of which was never to be opened before the first one was hermetically sealed and the temperature had dropped. The ice collected in winter was stacked there between layers of straw which provided enough insulation to keep it for five years. This ice was used to preserve foods without having to resort to salting, which spoilt the taste, as well as to cool drinks in the summer. To do this, the ice was place in *rafraîchissoirs* (coolers), marble basins like those dating from the time of Louis XV which are on display in the Cotelle Gallery in the Grand Trianon, where Louis-Philippe installed them for banquets. The ice was also used for sorbets, which were made in *sarbotières* (the term *sorbetière* dates from the 19th century), double-bottomed porcelain recipients: it was placed on the first bottom with sugar or sea salt which reacted, icing the fruit liqueurs placed in the second bottom. The flavor of these "snows" lay in the variety of fruit—oranges, peaches, plums, apples, redcurrants...—from the domain's crops, or in the vanilla, saffron, cloves, and chocolate imported from exotic countries.

# A BUCOLIC
# HERMITAGE

**\*ROUND ROOM**
FRENCH PAVILION

\*\* Menagerie of the Petit Trianon, adjoining the French garden, architect: Jacques Ange Gabriel

Children's games are depicted on the panels above the doors, evoking hunting, fishing, and gardening, mixed in with ducks, swans, roosters, and chickens in the paneled cornice, making up the admirable interior decor of the French Pavilion in which Louis XV liked to relax. After his long walks in his new horticultural domain and kitchen garden at the Trianon, the king came here for a coffee or a glass of strawberry milk, prepared in the adjoining rooms. From his work table where he classified his herbaria, he could look out towards the vistas of the garden *allées* where water spurted from little animal fountains. The decor was majestic but tempered by the simplicity of the low furniture, in harmony with the surrounding nature which Jacques Ange Gabriel strived to make as gentle as possible.

Created by Jacques Verbeckt and Antoine Rousseau in 1750, the panels were not originally gilded, but a very soft light green which went perfectly with the little bucolic scenes. Louis XV had chosen to have animals depicted to echo the menagerie which he had built in 1749, inspired by Madame de Pompadour's rural hermitages, which included a farm for barnyard animals, cows, and sheep. Opening onto the *allée* with the fountain depicting children playing with ducks, it was in direct view of the French Pavilion, which was called the Pavilion of the New Menagerie at the time. You can still see it on the north side of the garden, although it is now unfortunately separated by a wall.

\* Interior of the French Pavilion.

# THE GARDEN OF THE FOUR SEASONS

**COOL ROOM (RESTORATION BASED ON THE WORK BY JACQUES ANGE GABRIEL)**
PETIT TRIANON

The recent restoration of the Cool Room, where one sought the cool in summer, reinforces the symbolic nature of the French Garden of the Petit Trianon. Created by Jacques Ange Gabriel between 1750 and 1752, the landscaping reveals a learned allegory of the seasons and the elements. Laid out in the shape of a Greek cross, each of whose arms represents a season, the Round Room of the French Pavilion sits in the middle of the garden. The cross is intersected by the intermediate axes of the four corner rooms of the pavilion facing four parterres which once featured floral compositions, also thematic. Of this design, you can still make out the circle of the outer *allée* of the parterres which surrounded the pavilion, representing the sun cycle, with its

solstices and equinoxes, and the eternal renewal of the seasons. On the pavilion's façades, the decoration is sculpted with specific attributes, notably on the balustrade with its pairs of allegorical children. The west is devoted to fall, with children harvesting grapes or hunting; the north, facing the menagerie, to winter, with children fishing or warming themselves with a brazier; the east, facing the Petit Trianon, to spring, with children and flowers or birds; and the south, facing the Cool Room, to summer, with children harvesting or carrying a basket of fruit. Another curiosity of this harmonious ensemble is the *allée* leading from the Grand to the Petit Trianon, called "Allée des Evergreen." Linking the gardens of Louis XIV and Louis XV, it follows the axis corresponding to the fall equinox, planted with evergreens, as its name suggests. Here, the use of the English word "evergreen" is evidence of the Romantic landscaping which was to become dominant at the end of the century.

*Sculpted Children* (1750), by Jules-Antoine Rousseau, French Pavilion, east façade.

# THE RICHARDS
## AT WORK

**\*\* RICHARD HOUSE, A.K.A. "JUSSIEU PAVILION"**
PETIT TRIANON

Behind the menagerie lies the house of gardener Claude Richard and his son Antoine, great organizers of the grounds of the Petit Trianon. The father set up house there in 1751, according to the wishes of Louis XV and Madame de Pompadour, who had learned of his talents through the Duke de Noailles. Thanks to parcels of grains and live plants from the four corners of the Earth, to Antoine's botanizing voyages in the Balearic Islands, Spain, and Portugal, and to the assistance of Bernard de Jussieu, the Richards constituted the most extraordinary botanical collection in Europe: more than 4,000 exotic varieties acclimated in hothouses. This is how pineapples were grown for the first time in France. Louis XV was involved in this scientific adventure, classifying the plants with the help of the Richards who corresponded with Swedish naturalist Carolus Linnaeus. The king even founded a botanical school at Trianon before asking Jacques Ange Gabriel in 1762 to create the little palace we now know so as to be able to fully devote himself to his research.

Upon the king's death, Marie-Antoinette, who took possession of the domain, saved this patiently nurtured treasure. Demolishing the greenhouses to install her English garden, she asked the Richards to transfer the rare and exotic plants to the King's Garden in Paris (now the Jardin des Plantes). The gardeners themselves remained with the queen. Claude died at the Petit Trianon in 1784 while Antoine stayed on well past the Revolution, even managing to save Versailles' park from being auctioned off. He came up with the idea of planting fruit trees and vegetables there to feed the city's inhabitants.

# CULINARY
## MAGIC

**GRAND DINING ROOM**
PETIT TRIANON

I n Louis XV's time, this enfilade of rooms was a tasting lab for the fruits and vegetables grown at the Petit Trianon. The rich woods and paintings in the grand dining room celebrated the domain's abundance. The panels feature the mythological couples Boreas and Orythia, Flora and Zephyrus, Venus and Adonis, and Vertumnus and Pomona, while in four large paintings—*The Harvest, The Hunt, The Grape Harvest*, and *Fishing*—, nude nymphs and *putti* glorify the sources of all food. This representational sensuality is a veritable ode to nature. However, beauty doesn't always coexist well with artifice: in 1770, Louis XV commissioned inventor Antoine-Joseph Loriot to build three flying tables which were meant to surge up in the center of the room, loaded with dishes, using an ingenious system of pulleys and counterweights and rose-sculpted metal plaques that slid under the parquet floor! Marie-Antoinette, who inherited the domain in 1774, doesn't seem to have pursued this commission, even though we can see the masonry that was to house the mechanism in the basement of the fruitery on the ground floor. The only "magic tables" of Louis XV's reign were those in the Château de Choisy, created in 1756 by engineer Guérin de Montpellier. The legend of

these tables stoked the pamphlets which targeted the mistresses. The desire for an absence of domestics was criticized, and the worst orgies imagined. In fact, this theatrical dining presentation is more a mark of the culinary refinement of the 18th century.

** Site for the "flying table" mechanism, basement of the Petit Trianon

# THE SCENT
# OF A BOUQUET

**"EARS OF WHEAT" FURNITURE IN THE QUEEN'S CHAMBER (1787)**
PETIT TRIANON

In 1774, Louis XVI gave Marie-Antoinette a passkey set with 531 diamonds, telling her lovingly, "You love flowers, I have a bouquet for you, it's the Petit Trianon." The queen did love flowers, and more particularly drawing them with the "Raphael of flowers," Pierre Joseph Redouté. She called on many other artists to create the most exceptional applications in the design of her clothes and furniture, as evidenced by the polychrome "ears of wheat" ensemble she ordered in 1787 from cabinetmaker Georges Jacob for her bedroom in the Petit Trianon. The seats and screen sculpted with wicker, ears of wheat, jasmine, lily-of-the-valley, and pine cones, covered with a fabric embroidered with roses and cornflowers (her favorite flowers) are extraordinarily real, giving the illusion that the flowers are climbing around the wood. While Marie-Antoinette's tastes tended toward clean lines and white backgrounds, pastel tones like sea green, lilac, pearl gray, and pink, they also embraced these realistic floral fantasies. Her passion for flowers extended to perfumes. Her artisan in these matters, perfumer Jean-Louis Fargeon, developed light new scents for her, with a base of rose, violet, carnation, iris, jonquil, jasmine, and lily, which she used to perfume her clothes and her powders. The Petit Trianon itself had a special perfume with calming qualities made from orange blossom petals mixed with lavender, bergamot, and citron.

# LIVING
# PAINTINGS

**QUEEN'S BOUDOIR**
PETIT TRIANON

I n the room where Louis XV had coffee facing the greenhouses of his botanical garden, Marie-Antoinette set up a boudoir, a place from which she had an excellent view of her new English garden. She could also admire the work she had created between 1776 and 1783 with her advisers, the Count of Caraman and Hubert Robert, and her architect, Richard Mique. The clever mobile woodwork fitted with "movable mirrors" created by mechanist Jean-Tobie Mercklein date from this period; they rose from the ground floor where the mechanism is still visible. Symbolizing her desire for privacy, the moving mirrors were also tricks which allowed her to change the views of the outside. She unveiled veritable panoramas

chosen according to the fancy of the day, like a painter choosing paintings to set on his easel. All landscaping elements—the subtle compositions of trees, the sinuous carpets of lawn, the punctuations of uneven ground—varied depending on the weather and the light. At sunrise and sunset, evaporation off the lake and the river created effects of atmospheric depth which gave the landscape its romantic character. Like the frames of the large-paned windows, the new woodwork created by the Frères Rousseau in 1787—slender rose branches and white arabesques on a blue-gray linen back-ground—was meant to blend into the decor to better complement poetic musing.

# THE TWISTS AND TURNS OF LOVE

***CUPID CUTTING HIS BOW FROM THE CLUB OF HERCULES*** (1778)
COPY AFTER EDMÉ BOUCHARDON
TEMPLE OF LOVE
PETIT TRIANON

Commissioned by Louis XV in 1738, Cupid by Edmé Bouchardon was meant to be placed in the center of the Hercules Room of the Palace. However, during its installation in 1749, many people protested, his daughters in particular, denouncing its nudity and adolescent sensuality. So, the king decided to place the statue in the orangerie of the Château de Choisy. Madame de Pompadour, who liked the statue, had a copy made and installed in the Grove of Love of her Château de Bellevue. The dauphine Marie-Antoinette was not immune to the beauty of the work either. When in 1774 Louis XVI gave Louis XV's daughters the Château de Bellevue, it seems they got rid of the copy. Marie-Antoinette then decided to move the original to the Louvre to protect it, while making sure to ask Louis-Philippe Mouchy for another copy, for she had finally found the right statue for her garden. To show it off to its best advantage, she decided to place it in the center of a round temple, a marble tholos with twelve Corinthian columns, built by Richard Mique in 1778 and modeled on the classical Temple of Vesta in Rome. Sheltered under a magnificent cupola featuring one hundred and twenty rosette coffers, with a keystone adorned with a trophy of Cupid with his attributes, the work became the perfect symbol of the quest for happiness advocated by the Enlightenment, in opposition to the glory of Herculean values.

# THE GUARDIANS
## OF HARMONY

**THE BELVEDERE OR THE ROCK PAVILION**
PETIT TRIANON

Four pairs of female sphinxes (fantastic winged creatures, half woman, half lion) are set on the four staircases leading to the circular flight of stairs up to the octagonal pavilion where Marie-Antoinette liked to listen to music and observe nature awakening in the spring, running her eyes over the parterres of myrtle, roses, and jasmine which covered the slopes to the lake. Remember, Œdipus vanquished the female sphinx sent by Hera to punish the peasants of Thebes for their trickery, by answering her riddle and forcing her to throw herself off a cliff. In the queen's music pavilion, the different attributes of the sphinxes sculpted by Joseph Deschamps are clues which allow us to solve their riddles by guessing their symbolic function: wreaths of flowers, Egyptian headdresses adorned with ears of wheat, vines and reeds, and classical draperies each represent a season.

Sculpted on the pediments of the French doors of the Belvedere are four corresponding rural scenes, while the bas-reliefs of the four corner bays feature spring with Flora crowned with roses, summer with Ceres, her head ringed with ears of wheat, fall with Bacchus and vines, and winter with Saturn warming himself by a fire.

Along the cornice, there runs a frieze of garlands of fruit and flowers, once in painted colors, which form a loop symbolizing the cycle of time and the seasons. So these sphinxes are indeed the guardians of this little pavilion in harmony with nature, where men's destructive passions are forbidden.

# REVERIES OF
# A SOLITARY WALKER

**ENTRANCE TO MARIE-ANTOINETTE'S GROTTO**
PETIT TRIANON

On October 5, 1789, as a crowd of Parisian women trespassed on Versailles, Marie-Antoinette was in her grotto at the Petit Trianon, receiving Monsieur de Saint-Priest's letter reminding her of reality. Located near the Belvedere, this artificial grotto, where the queen could watch for arriving visitors thanks to a little chink in the wall, was not just a picturesque retreat. It was also the materialization of an ideal of simple and authentic life in nature, as advocated by Enlightenment philosophers like Jean-Jacques Rousseau in *Reveries of a Solitary Walker* (1776–1778). The staging of this wild nature, with its grasses and mossy trees, its rambling paths bordered with brambles, its torrents and waterfalls, brought to mind Alpine landscapes and the atmosphere of another of Rousseau's novels, *Julie, or the New Heloise* (1761) where the heroine, out of loyalty, marries the man her father has chosen, but does not break ties with her tutor, whom she loves.

Doing what society demands without giving up her "secret principles" and the feelings which govern deep identity—such could have been Marie-Antoinette's private motto.

# IN THE QUEEN'S
## PRIVATE SPACE

**\* MADAME CAMPAN'S BEDROOM**
PETIT TRIANON

On the second floor of the Petit Trianon, above Marie-Antoinette's, there are the rooms reserved for her two main servants: the lady-in-waiting, the Princess of Chimay, and the first lady-in-waiting in charge of her toilet and dressing, the Baroness de Misery. In 1786, Madame Campan, who was to become famous for her memoirs, succeeded the latter. In a world where birth counted above all else, this commoner had an exceptional life. While her human qualities earned her the queen's affection, Madame Campan mainly owed her fortune to her father, the First Clerk for Foreign Affairs; his position got her into court as a reader to the daughters of Louis XV. In 1770, she was placed in the house of the Dauphine as the second lady-in-waiting. As Louis XV had granted her a dowry, she married François Bertholet-Campan, whose father was to become Marie-Antoinette's secretary and librarian, and above all the stage manager of her theater at the Petit Trianon. She was therefore witness to the queen's private moments, and it is thanks to her famous memoirs, published posthumously in 1822, that Marie-Antoinette was seen in a new light. However, Madame Campan was already known for her treatises on education and her defense of the cause of women. In 1794, in Madame de Maintenon's footsteps, she had founded a boarding school for young girls in Saint-Germain-en-Laye. She then ran the Maison Impériale school in Écouen for the daughters of the Officers of the Légion d'Honneur. Nonetheless, she lived her last years in poverty, after her school was closed by Louis XVIII who reproached her for her affinities with the Napoleonic regime.

# COMEDY
# OR TRAGEDY?

**QUEEN'S THEATER**

The two female figures guarding the entrance to Marie-Antoinette's theater tell spectators to expect heights of eloquence and satire in the pure tradition of Greek theater. Melpomene, muse of singing, musical harmony, and tragedy, holds a scepter and a dagger, and Thalia, muse of comedy, accompanied by a cherub armed with a shepherd's satchel, holds a flute and a mask. It is here that the queen invited her "society" to perform festive and playful theater pieces, like *The Unforeseen Wager* or *The King and the Farmer* by Michel Jean Sedaine, or *The Village Soothsayer* by Jean-Jacques Rousseau, a play in which she played the shepherdess Colette. As a young princess in the Viennese court, she had performed with her family, perfecting her French and taking acting lessons. At Versailles, she turned her back on the representational performance imposed on her by the court, saving her acting skills for this theater where she wanted to feel at home, surrounded by a select audience. Sometimes she even enjoyed performing in front of her servants, who must have been a great audience. Her last known role, on September 15, 1785, was Rosine in *The Barber of Seville* by Beaumarchais, who was

in attendance. The controversy which was to plague the second installment of the play was of no importance to Marie-Antoinette. In *The Marriage of Figaro*, Beaumarchais gave Figaro a few prophetic words criticizing the privileges of the nobility: "What have you done to have so much? You took the trouble to be born, nothing more." Doubtless the queen only realized too late the subversive power of theater which had the means to make people laugh so.

Allegory at the entrance to the Queen's Theater.

# SELECT
# SURPRISES PARTIES

**SITE OF THE "CHINESE RING GAME"**
PETIT TRIANON, NORTHWEST CORNER

At the entrance to the pergola of the Petit Trianon's garden there is a vast circular lawn bordered by hedges. It calls to mind the "Chinese ring game" which Marie-Antoinette ordered in 1776 from the Menus-Plaisirs—specifically from sculptor Augustin Bocciardi—modeled on that of the Duke of Chartres in Monceau. This took the form of a merry-go-round with a giant umbrella turning on a pivot. Perched on dragons alternating with four peacocks, players used long sticks to try to remove rings hung from posts. Illustrating the queen's taste for games, it was part of the backdrop of the celebrations she organized. The first such party was held on September 4, 1777: the ladies were disguised as merchants and the queen as a café owner.

Lit by flares, the grounds of the Petit Trianon were transformed for the occasion into a funfair dotted with temporary structures, rustic pavilions made of leaves, Turkish tents, and Chinese kiosks. Choirs and

orchestras played under the trees, while the lake reflected the dancing lights of Venetian lanterns hung from the boats.

These enchanting spectacles were captured in the 1781 painting by Claude-Louis Châtelet. Only a privileged few were invited, under assumed names, from a list the queen herself drew up for the concierge of the domain. These private festivities put the noses of snubbed courtiers out of joint and rumors flared. Outdoor entertainments weren't new at Versailles, but their being made private went against the tradition whereby they were public events and signs of royal bliss.

*Illumination of the Belvedere at the Petit Trianon (1781),* by Claude-Louis Châtelet.

# COUNTRY
# AIR

This warming room was used to warm dishes from the kitchens of the Petit Trianon, leaving the fireplace free for other uses, such as lighting embers or heating water. Its decor is false, for these thatched buildings were based on a mere illusion of rusticity: walls painted to look like cut stone, fake wood, fake lizards... However, the interiors of most of the other little houses in the Hamlet which were used by the queen herself, like the billiard room or the boudoir, were truly luxuriously furnished. This is why they were called "surprise cottages." Rambouillet, to the south of Paris, has a perfectly preserved example in the Princess of Lamballe's Shell Cottage. Marie-Antoinette, who envied it, asked Richard Mique to build her the Hamlet in 1783; the architect had just created cottages in Bellevue for the daughters of Louis XV. The first example of these garden follies, inspired by traditional seventeenth-century Flemish painting, was created by Jean-François Leroy in 1774 in Chantilly for the Prince of Condé. Nevertheless, Richard Mique built an ensemble of unprecedented scale at the Petit Trianon. A complete landscape, the Hamlet invites dreaming, as it comes straight out of the imagination of the travel accounts and multiple engravings of the day, such as those made by painter Claude-Louis Châtelet to accompany *Picturesque Voyage or Description of the Kingdoms of Naples and Sicily* (1781–1786) by the Abbot of Saint-Non. The queen also commissioned this painter to paint views of her Hamlet, which she presented in album form to her guests, as a souvenir of their picturesque stay in an idealized countryside.

# MOTHER NATURE'S ETIQUETTE

**\*\* BALCONY OF THE QUEEN'S HOUSE**
QUEEN'S HAMLET
PETIT TRIANON

When in 1775 Marie-Antoinette named her friend the Princess of Lamballe superintendent of her house, the Countess de Noailles, whom she had pejoratively dubbed "Madame Étiquette," was forced to leave that post. The queen could no longer stand stifling court customs and aspired to the free lifestyle she enjoyed in her Hamlet at the Petit Trianon. Guests invited to spend the day there had to be natural: for women, light clothing, percale dresses in light colors, gauze shawls, straw hats and loose hair were in order, and for men, a simple jacket. Activities amounted to playing ball and boules on the lawn, punting on the lake, and reading in the shade of the trees... This tranquility could only be stirred by the sounds of mandolins and guitars. All the doors of the cottages had to be wide open so people could come and go with ease. The queen ordered that no one rise when she entered a room, because she didn't want to be reminded of her rank. She encouraged her guests to converse in all sincerity and to remember the moralist apologies of the *Fables* by Claris de Florian, elevated to the rank of principles. By setting a frank tone quite foreign to the manners of Versailles, Marie-Antoinette upheld the spirit of a very different etiquette, in perfect harmony with the apparent simplicity of the "surprise cottages" whose interiors were nonetheless extremely refined.

# A GENTLE WHITE
## BILLY GOAT

**\*\* QUEEN'S HAMLET**
PETIT TRIANON

The Hamlet was no mere operetta backdrop, since each of the houses had a working kitchen garden. Running along the *allées* there were orchards, grape vines, and tilled fields where rye, barley, oats, buckwheat, and peas were grown. A little way off, there was a farm, put into service in 1785, which opened onto the pastures all the way to the woods. The operation was run by an oxherd from Touraine, Valy Bussard, his wife and two children, as well as by a young cowherd called Gaëtan. The herd included cows from Switzerland, including two, Brunette and Blanchette, which were the royal family's favorites, a bull, calves, chickens, a pig, as well as goats and a four-horned billy goat which the queen had requested be "white and gentle." Regardless of the song "Il pleut, il pleut bergère" (It's raining, it's raining, shepherdess), there were no sheep.

This nursery rhyme, written in 1780 by Fabre d'Églantine for the operetta *Laure et Pétrarque*, did not in fact refer to the queen. This did not stop perverse minds from embroidering viciously on this upper aristocracy venturing into stable muck, racing pell-mell to catch rabbits and amusing themselves with straw battles. For the royal family however, it was an attempt to reconnect with the reality of rural France. The farm at the Hamlet could be compared to a laboratory. Like Antoine Laurent de Lavoisier, who on his lands took an interest in subsistence problems, agricultural yields, and crop diversification, Louis XVI was a physiocratic king. His agricultural philosophy was not very different from the policies of Henry IV and his famous *poule au pot* (chicken stew) when, for example, he became the ardent defender of Antoine Parmentier's potato.

# CURES
# AND WHEY

**DAIRY**
QUEEN'S HAMLET
PETIT TRIANON

I n the dairy's cottage, the farm's dairy products one sampled. In porcelain from the Rue Thiroux in Paris, Marie-Antoinette was served cream produced in the dairy, freshly churned buttermilk, cheese from her cows and goats, and whey, which was said to have curative virtues. She had doubtless gleaned this fashionable diet advice from the accounts of travelers who, passing through the Appenzell or the Grisons, were offered this precious beverage in the villages. Even at the Tuileries prison after 1789, the queen received little pots of butter from her farmer Valy Bussard. This search for a healthy life is evoked in the unpretentious decor of the dairy, with its light-colored *trompe-l'œil* stones. Nonetheless, most of the decorative elements date from the 19<sup>th</sup> century, and the original marble furniture created by Le Prince in 1786 has disappeared. It was Aimable Boischard who, in 1811, starting restoration of the dairy at Napoleon's request, ordered the grand marble table, on which Louis XVIII substituted an "L" for the "N," as well as the wall basins with the dolphins and ibexes which replaced the queen's, which had been made of hard-paste porcelain and stylized with a pattern of cornflowers and gold lace. The water which arrived from the reservoir installed in the roof space was however never connected to the fountains, even if it circulated in the channel fitted under the marble-tiled floor, making the room pleasantly cool during the hot days of summer.

# A TOWER FOR TACKLE

## ** FISHING TOWER, A.K.A. MARLBOROUGH TOWER
### QUEEN'S HAMLET
### PETIT TRIANON

This romantic little tower, built by Richard Mique in 1783 and located on the edge of the carp pond of the Hamlet, was where the royal family's fishing equipment was stored. Inspired by the lighthouses of the Mediterranean coast, it was capped with a belvedere overlooking the domain. It is said to have been given the name "Marlborough Tower" in reference to the song "Malbrough s'en va t'en guerre," popularized by Beaumarchais and which Marie-Antoinette played on the harpsichord. The First Dauphin's nurse, Geneviève Poitrine, hummed this nursery rhyme for the queen's children, which is no doubt how the Hamlet tower their mother climbed earned its name. The song tells of a certain Lady Malbrough, all dressed in pink, watching every day for the return of her beloved. One day, a page comes to tell her that her beloved has died and that a nightingale is singing on his grave to celebrate his soul's flight through the laurels. The soldier in the song was not fictional: it was John Churchill, Duke of Marlborough, wounded in the Battle of Malplaquet in 1709 during the Spanish War of Succession. During the American War of Independence, the duke's frenzied struggle came to symbolize the animosity of the "perfidious Albion" on which revenge had to be taken. The Seven Years' War, which had led to the birth of the British Empire, was still a vivid memory, and despite the royal family's Anglophilia, an *entente cordiale* did not yet reign.

# A FORGOTTEN TEMPLE OF LOVE

**TEMPLE OF LOVE**
PETIT TRIANON

In the heart of the English garden, near the Temple of Love on the way to the Hamlet, there flows ferruginous water rediscovered by fountaineers during recent restoration work. In Marie-Antoinette's time, the water was channeled and spilled into a grotto, which is now gone. The queen drank this water for its therapeutic virtues every day, and wanted her children to do the same. The Petit Trianon was not a solitary paradise, but rather a family domain where Marie-Antoinette could supervise her children's education. Far from the drawing rooms of Versailles, she tried to train them to study nature and guide them in the practice of a healthy country life, according to the principles set out by Jean-Jacques Rousseau in his treatise *Émile, or On Education* (1762). To her great pleasure, her second son, Louis Charles, born in 1785, was, in her words, "a real farm boy, fresh and plump."

However, despite her best efforts, Marie-Antoinette would be unable to skirt tragedy: she lost two of her four children, Sophie Béatrice in 1787 at the age of 11 months and the dauphin Louis Joseph, her "dearest love," in 1789 at the age of 7 from bone tuberculosis. The sovereigns barely had time to mourn his death, because the Estates General were in session at Versailles. The dauphin, born to great rejoicing, died to general indifference, heralding the end of the monarchy.

*Marie-Antoinette Walking with Madame Royale and the Dauphin in the English Garden* (1868), by Eugène Bataille, after a work by Adolf Ulrik Wertmüller.

# VERSAILLES, THE PALACE, ITS PARK, AND THE CITY

● THE CITY
● THE PARK

1. Grande Écurie
2. Petite Écurie
3. Water Parterre
4. Latona Fountain
5. Apollo Fountain
6. Grove of the Colonnade
7. King's Garden
8. Grove of the Girandole
9. Ballroom
10. Queen's Grove (former Labyrinth)
11. Orangerie
12. Grove of Apollo's Baths
13. Grove of the Three Fountains
14. Grove of the Arc de Triomphe
15. Dragon Fountain
16. Neptune Fountain
17. Grove of the Obelisk
18. Grove of Enceladus
19. Little Venice
20. Site of the former Royal Menagerie
21. Gally Farm
22. Grand Trianon
23. Allée des Hâ-Hâ
24. Petit Trianon
25. French Pavilion
26. House of the gardener Richard
27. Ice houses on the Trianon domain
28. Queen's Hamlet

29. Farm of the Queen's Hamlet
30. Saint-Antoine Gate
31. Water Tower
32. House of Madame de Pompadour
33. Montansier Theater
34. Ermitage of Madame de Pompadour
35. Guet du Roy
36. Queen's Stables, now the Appeals Courts of Versailles
37. Pavillon des Sources
38. Notre-Dame Church
39. Lambinet Museum
40. Notre-Dame marketplace
41. Entranceway of the Church of the Récollets
42. Grand Commun
43. Hôtel de la Marine et des Affaires Étrangères, now the municipal library
44. Swiss Lake
45. King's Kitchen Garden
46. Saint-Louis Cathedral
47. Carrés Saint-Louis
48. Museum of the Revolution (Tennis Room)
49. Hôtel de la Chancellerie, currently the Regional Conservatory for Music, Dance, and Dramatic Arts

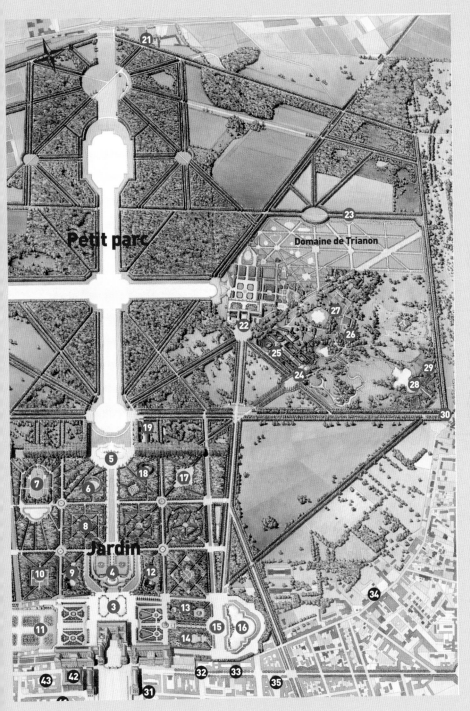

Petit parc

Domaine de Trianon

Jardin

# CENTRAL BODY OF THE PALACE
## GROUND FLOOR

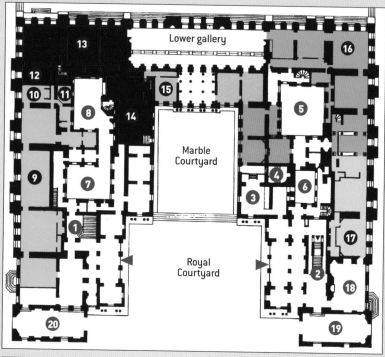

Apartment of the Dauphin
Apartment of the Dauphine
Apartment of Madame Victoire

Apartment of Madame Adélaïde
Apartment for the Captain of the Guards
Queen's Small Apartment

**1**. Queen's Staircase
**2**. Marshals' Staircase (former site of the Ambassadors' Staircase)
**3**. Small King's Guards' Room
**4**. King's Small Staircase
**5**. Courtyard of the Stags
**6**. King's Small Courtyard
**7**. Monsieur's Courtyard
**8**. Queen's Courtyard
**9**. Grand Cabinet of the Dauphine
**10**. Cabinet of the Dauphine, with niche

**11**. Bathroom of the Duchess of Angoulême
**12**. Library of the Dauphin
**13**. Bedroom of the Dauphin
**14**. Guards' Room
**15**. Queen's Bathroom
**16**. Grand Cabinet of Madame Victoire
**17**. Grand Cabinet of Madame Adélaïde
**18**. Provost Guards' Room
**19**. Passage to the North Parterre
**20**. Passage to the South Parterre

# SECOND FLOOR

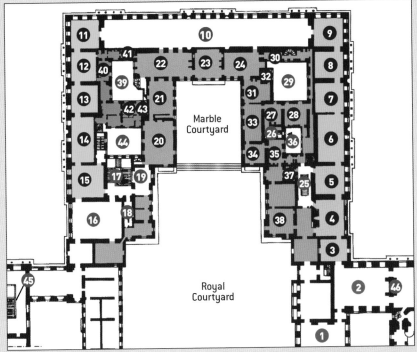

Marble Courtyard

Royal Courtyard

# DETAILED LIST OF ENTRIES

## VERSAILLES, THE PARK ...... 133